Tails from a Greek Mountainside

by

Guy Hanley

AN ANALOGUE WARMTH
PUBLICATION

Tails from a Greek Mountainside

by

Guy Hanley

Originally published 2022

Second edition published 2022 by

Analogue Warmth

Photography by Guy and Anne Hanley

Extra special thanks go to ...

Anne for absolutely everything ... Steve Potz-Rayner, Craig Coward, Abi Cullimore, Theresa Stoker for proofreading ...Philip Buckley-Mellor for the cover ... Paul Kenney for help with publishing ... and to all the people who read this.

About The Author

Guy Hanley was born and raised in Reading, Berkshire, UK (1974). He travelled extensively in south east Asia, hitchhiking there and through both islands of New Zealand before studying Economics and French at Birmingham University. Armed with a thoroughly average Economics degree he then studied and completed a Law degree, also at Birmingham University, before realising that he hated law, and ended up working in finance until 18 months after the global financial crisis hit.

He married Anne, born in Sunderland in 1965, on the same day that Michael Jackson died in 2009, losing front page headlines as a result. They honeymooned in Kefalonia, a place they had fallen in love with five years previously, visiting every year afterwards, starting their love affair with Greece.

Guy is obsessed with music and plays bass guitar for Barefoot Rock & Blues with Chris and Steve, a covers band who have a weekly residency outside at Patriko bar in Stoupa Bay during tourist season.

He adores animals of all sorts, mountain hiking, mosaics, growing fruit and vegetables and also cooking.

3. Pastitsio

4. Souvlaki

5. Kolokythes Keftades (Fried Courgette Balls)

6. Spetsofai

7. Briam

To the Memory

of

Certain Animal Companions

who

While this Work was being Completed

were

Constantly by the Author's Side

Not only in the Garden

but

At his Desk by the Pool

Giving to his Words

The approval of their muted Purrs and Barks

and

The Authority of their Muddy Paws

Adapted from a dedication by Beverley Nichols from the book
'Garden Open Tomorrow' (1968).

Foreword

One of my favourite cartoons was featured in Private Eye magazine, with two men at a drinks party.

Man One: *'Actually, I'm currently writing a book'.*

Man Two: *'You're writing a book? Neither am I!'*

It is July 2020 and I'm furloughed from work. I've 'threatened' to write a book about our experiences in Greece for many years, so I figured it was 'now or never'. So this is it; all of it. It is not all 'blue sky and black olives', it is dark at times unfortunately, but it is honest and true. It covers the decade 2010-2020, our decision to move to Greece, our successes and many failures and the animals that accompanied us on our adventure.

When we arrived in Greece we wanted to live a more simple life, to grow our own vegetables, keep chickens and become as self-sufficient as possible. We wanted to learn the language and understand Greek culture as well as explore the country. We wanted to sample Greek food, taking fresh ingredients we had grown ourselves and to learn how to cook authentic Greek dishes, recreated from tavernas we had visited.

After renting for several years we now own our own house, set in a nice amount of land overlooking the Mediterranean. We are largely self-sufficient for fruit and vegetables with a polytunnel for all year growing and five years ago we planted an olive grove, with olives to press for oil and also to eat. The fruit trees we planted are maturing nicely, so at various times of the year we get olives, peaches, grapefruit, oranges, tangerines, lemons, limes, apples and also grapes. Our chickens provide us, friends and neighbours with the best eggs I have ever tasted.

We both speak and write Greek, not to an amazing standard, but we get by.

After much trial and error I can cook most of the classic Greek dishes we love from the tavernas and later I will share my recipes with you for you to try.

Lastly, and very importantly, we both have residency, which will now be needed due to Brexit. We got in just as the door was closing to people not already resident in the EU.

When we first came over we had 'just' four animals to our name, all cats. Now we have … well, let's just say 'a good few more than that'. This is their story as much as ours, but it is not solely a story about Greece and animals. Yes, it is mostly a love story to a country that has taken us in and the animals that we have adopted along the way, but it is also a story of a couple emigrating from London in their mid-30s/40s and the difficulties they have faced and overcome.

When researching this book I read a comment on a local forum from someone who said 'I love all books about Greece, I read them all, even the tedious ramblings of ex-pats'. I class myself as an immigrant rather than an ex-pat, but either way, I hope my writing doesn't fall into the latter category and I hope you enjoy this rollercoaster as much as we all have.

Most importantly, I'd like to give my never-ending thanks to my wife, Anne, who has been my partner, co-pilot, partner in crime, confidant, nurse and best friend over all these years.

Chapter One: 'Sod It, Shall We Just Move to Greece?'

Anne and I first met at work in 2004 and married in 2009. We lived in North London in an Edwardian maisonette that we had renovated together and had four cats. We both worked in central London, Anne as a Personal Assistant and I worked in finance. London life was fun and we both enjoyed our jobs for the most part. We ate out lots, met up with friends, went to loads of gigs and each rode a Vespa to avoid having to use the Tube.

The two downsides of London were the weather and our health. Winters seemed to go on forever, with just a few months available for growing vegetables on our small terrace. We lived an unhealthy indoor life with little exercise and a poor diet. Like most Brits, we lived for holidays and had particularly fallen for the Greek island of Kefalonia. As a rule we never went away to the same place twice, but we kept on going back to Kefalonia. We couldn't keep away, visiting six times and indeed went there for our honeymoon in 2009.

The 2008 banking crisis changed everything. My job outlook was shaky to say the least and we began looking for alternatives - alternative jobs and also perhaps an alternative life altogether. For a while we toyed with the idea of moving to Koh Chang, a small island on the border between Thailand and Cambodia, but when we visited again with our 'sensible heads' on as opposed to our 'holiday heads' it just didn't work - it was too wild, too lawless, too far away, plus I wasn't sure I could handle the humidity and heavy rains of the monsoon season.

My overall boss, a lovely, yet fiery, Italian brought up in New York, was based in Rome and sometimes we would go weeks without communicating as he just let me do my thing. I quickly figured out I could redirect my phone and take as much holiday as I wanted - I think I managed 12 weeks in 2009. Why not there was nothing else happening. This plan was helped by the fact that Anne had just changed jobs after we got married and so had a full holiday entitlement.

One day in September 2009 at work I was idly surfing the web and spotted a holiday deal from the same company through which we booked our holidays to Kefalonia - a week on the Greek mainland in a place called Stoupa. I'd never heard of it before, nor did I realise precisely what a life changing moment this would be. I called Anne: 'fancy another nice holiday in Greece?'

We flew out a week or so later to Kalamata airport. Kalamata was a place I had heard of due to its olives, but that was the full extent of my knowledge. Then there was a hair raising one hour taxi ride up one side of a mountain and down the other side. Our villa was right on Kalogria beach, possibly the most beautiful beach in Southern mainland Greece. Stoupa itself was a crescent bay full of charming bars and tavernas and a short, 5 minute walk away. The Taygetos Mountains loomed in the background and fed cold water springs that popped up in the sea, so one moment you are swimming in beautiful, warm, turquoise water and the next you hit an icy plume.

Stoupa was special. We met people who had been coming back here every year for 20 years. As I lay back in the sea looking at the majestic Taygetos, I said to Anne 'could you live here?'

The magic words came back - 'Oh yes'.

Back in cold England, life continued. November 18th 2009 was a fairly normal day at work - a bacon sandwich and tea at my desk, stupid jokes with my friends on the desk, not a lot of actual work and plans to meet Anne for lunch. As I went to the lift I spotted my London based boss Charles and the Head of HR chatting. Charles was a great guy, scarily intelligent, he reminded me of Dr Emmett Brown, the mad genius with the DeLorean in 'Back to the Future'. There had been several rounds of redundancies already and I believe I had been saved more than once by his intervention. I liked him a lot. As the lift went down he said 'You need to prepare for the worst I'm afraid'. The bullet with my name on had finally found me, so I met Anne, had a few drinks and told her the bad news, then found Gazz and Choccy, workmates from my desk, and we headed out to the pub for a further 3 bottles of wine. Being made redundant is not a lot of fun, I really wouldn't recommend it. But if it has to happen, at least face it very, very drunk.

I left with no bad blood and decided to take a few months off. As it happened, I was already fairly advanced in talks with another employer, a large domestic bank, so I picked up the pace of discussions. My friend who worked there had secured me an interview with the divisional head who had offered to take me out for lunch. I sat there in reception on Bishopsgate and waited. And waited. I called up to see if he had forgotten me to be told he had already left some 20 minutes previously. About ten minutes later my lunch date came back, flustered, and apologised. He had taken the wrong person to lunch and it was only after they had ordered that he asked 'so, why do you want to work in this area?' The chap replied that he was an IT specialist! This was not long after the BBC famously interviewed a taxi driver live on air rather than an industry expert. He was also called Guy - must be something in the name.

The lunch went well and he all but offered me a job there and then and said he would be in touch. A week passed and nothing. How long do you leave it before chasing up? I left it one more week and then sent a brief, but friendly email. Nothing. This was strange.

One morning in early March I woke up, checked my emails and there it was, just a very bland and short 'sorry, but there is nothing available right now, we wish you all the best'. It would take me five years to find out the reasons behind this rather strange episode.

I showed Anne the email. I still remember the exact discussion that followed:

Anne: 'That's a shame - sod it, shall we move to Greece?'

Me: 'Yeah!'

It really was that quick and that simple. I've recounted this story to so many people over the years and virtually no one has believed me, but that is the honest truth.

That was on a Tuesday. That day we booked our flights to Athens, booked the hire car and secured accommodation as well as setting up rental house viewings. As it was off-season we couldn't fly to Kalamata, so we had to fly to Athens and then faced a 5.5 hour drive to get to Stoupa after we landed. Friday we flew out and drove down. Saturday we looked at a number of houses. Sunday we signed a two year rental agreement, handed over the deposit, drove 5.5 hours back to Athens and flew home. Monday at 9am Anne resigned from her job. When we decide to do something we don't mess around!

We would pick up the keys to our new house, a three storey Mani Tower with roof access, on 1st May 2010.

Life was starting to get very interesting and very, very busy.

Chapter Two: 20 Pages of A4 Lists

Before she resigned, Anne was an Executive PA; she was adept at writing lists and organising. We very quickly amassed a 'To Do' list of approximately 20 pages of A4. Just the sight of it was daunting. We had to prepare the flat for rental, find a tenant, sort through our possessions and decide what to ship over, vaccinate the cats and then organise for them to be flown over. On top of that, I had a business idea for Anne to pitch to a former employer of hers, which she subsequently won, so we had to set up our own company.

The flat rented out quickly, thankfully. We had a viewing from a TV presenter who I will not name, but thankfully she didn't think the place was big enough, a relief as I'm sure she would have been the tenant from Hell. At one point she said 'is that your baby screaming?' I replied that I didn't have a baby, just four cats. It was at that point that she realised she had left her own baby in its pushchair at the bottom of the stairs. A lovely actress and her soap star boyfriend were also interested, but they pulled out about an hour before they were meant to sign on the dotted line. Had things turned out differently the winner's trophy from Strictly Come Dancing would have been displayed in our old London living room later that year.

Sorting through our possessions was cathartic (from the Greek word *'kathari'*, meaning clean). Most of our clothes went to the charity shop, including four of my suits; another sign that we were heading for a very different life. I kept one suit for weddings, but sadly it has since been used more for funerals.

We sold the rest of our stuff at two car boot sales. I'd never done one before, but loved it. At first I was not used to the haggling, but within an hour I was like Pete Beale, the market trader from Eastenders back in the day; *'owight darlin', take yerself up West and tweat yerself nice an' pwopa'*.

As our departure date drew near it was time to say goodbye to family and friends. I was careful in what I said to people, avoiding saying 'we're never coming back', just in case things went wrong. I was scared of coming back, having failed for whatever reason, with my tail between my legs, but as time has passed I realised that anybody trying this - successful or not - is to be congratulated. It's a big step. Sometimes for whatever reason things don't work, but just taking that first step is incredibly difficult.

We said goodbye to Anne's parents, who thought the whole idea was wonderful.

My final meal with my parents before Anne and I left the UK was at Hix Oyster and Chop House on the coast in Lyme Regis. After the meal as we got up to leave we saw a framed note with a sketch and on closer inspection it turned out to be a thank you note from a hero of mine, the chef Keith Floyd.

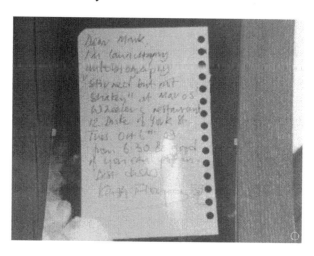

He had sat at the very table we had, ate a meal, went home and passed away the same night. From an early age I adored his shows, even though I didn't cook very much. The travel to exotic locations, the way he spoke to his cameraman, the anarchy. I've recently re-watched the entire back catalogue of shows and it is just as good as I remembered, a particular favourite being him eating tapas in La Boqueria market, Barcelona, where he drank a goldfish bowl sized glass of red wine at each stall with his food before moving on to the next, finally stumbling out several hours later absolutely legless.

We managed to get all the cats vaccinated and their pet passports completed. For their journey to Kalamata we employed a pet relocation service, which turned out to be money well spent and a large amount of stress avoided. The day before we left they came to pick the cats up, both Anne and I were in tears as they drove off, being very scared about whether they would make it to Greece alive, having read some horrible scare stories on the internet.

The house was now empty, just down to the bare bones of our possessions, with the removal firm clearing all of our stuff out in a matter of hours. All we had left were a mattress, a microwave, a kettle, a duvet and a few items of cutlery.

Our final job was to pack the car. As I turned on the ignition to move the car nearer to our house the engine kept cutting out. Even I, just about able to change a tyre and nothing more, knew something was badly wrong. Great, just 12 hours before we leave and the first problem I have ever had with that lovely reliable car rears its ugly head. I took it to a garage under the arches of the former railway line from Highgate to Alexandra Palace that ran behind our house and was told to call back in two hours. This could ruin all of our carefully laid out plans. I couldn't wait the full two hours, so I walked around to see him and he calmly said 'yeah, you need a new part, I've ordered it and it should be here in an hour'. I could have kissed him right there and then, but instead gave him a few nice bottles of wine when I settled the bill.

We had kept back essentials for the car, things that we would need before our shipment of possessions turned up, like bedding and clothes, plus some gardening equipment to get started on the vegetable patches, but we were seriously at our limit of how much we could fit in the car.

April 27th 2010 was our final night as UK residents. We celebrated by ordering a large Chinese takeaway and wine, eaten on makeshift tables fashioned from upturned cardboard boxes.

Chapter Three: The Road to Hellas

This really was the most fun, exciting journey of my life. It is just a shame that we had only planned three and a half days to complete the entire trip as I'd have loved to spend some more time in the places we raced through, but we had to be in Greece 1st May 2010 to meet the flight that the cats were arriving on in Kalamata.

We left at 3am to get an early crossing from Folkestone to Calais on the Eurostar Le Shuttle Train through the Channel Tunnel. Britain was heading into a General Election and Greece's economic woes were worsening by the day. As we left London we saw lots of extreme right wing political billboards and it depressed the hell out of me. I was glad to be leaving; UK politics had dragged me down since about 2001. Of course Greece has its fair share of extreme right wing politicians with Golden Dawn but as I hoped I could filter out their miserable existence.

At Folkestone we got bacon rolls for the swift journey through the tunnel and were in France by 8am.

The plan was to cross France to Switzerland, staying the night in Basel, where my brother, sister-in-law and two nieces lived. Noel, my younger brother, had worked for a pharmaceutical company for many years and his job first moved him to Hanover, then to Basel, where he still lives today.

This leg of the journey was long and tiring, but we switched driving duties every three or four hours, and finally arrived in Basel at around 4pm. Noel's house was gorgeous, 100 yards from the banks of the Rhine, with Germany on the other side of the river. We hadn't all seen each other for quite a while, so as Noel cooked, Rachel, my sister-in-law handed out drinks, while Anne and I played with my adorable nieces, Georgia and Evie. Their hospitality is legendary and I must admit that we took full advantage of it; too much really for a couple who were due to drive much of the way down Italy the next day.

Anne was due to do the early shift driving, but her head was hurting, so I lucked out and got the easy half of the journey to our destination for the night, Rimini, on the East coast of Italy. I drove through lovely empty Swiss roads, past snowy mountains, through tunnels - a LOT of tunnels - and then through the border and past the Italian lakes. The lakes really looked stunning; I really would recommend spending some time there and should we ever do this journey again that will be number one on my list.

Anne's half of the journey was far harder. The Italian drivers were crazy, and the average speed must have been 95mph, really aggressive. Of course we had yet to 'enjoy' the Greek style of driving, but for now this had me worried! However, Anne thankfully managed the drive without incident.

We arrived at the ancient city of Rimini at around 6pm and found our hotel. It was right on the beach, which was miles and miles of golden sand. I turned on BBC News to see how the election campaigning back in the UK was going, only to see that Gordon Brown had been caught with his microphone still on complaining that a bigoted lady who had harangued him was ... well, bigoted. He later had to go back, humiliated, and apologise to her, but by that time we guessed it was over for him.

Rimini has lovely Roman ruins, two thousand year old arches, a dog park (charmingly called 'Fido Park') and amazing food. We found a street café that had fixed price menu options of a main meal (meat/pasta), a bottle of wine and baklava for just €12 - we had earned it! That evening was the first time I had felt warm since our first visit to Stoupa, seven months previously, and I even got my pasty white legs out and wore some shorts.

The reason for choosing Rimini as an overnight stay is that the next stage of our journey was an overnight ferry from Ancona - just a few miles down the coast - to Patras in Greece. We arrived nice and early at the ticket office only to be told that our tickets were valid for the day before and not that day. 'Not a problem, on you go' said the friendly chap. Crisis averted.

We had booked a cabin, but many people just sleep on chairs on the boat or even out on the deck. Happy with our choice, we went for another large meal with wine and went to sleep knowing that the next day we would be in our new home and reunited with our cats.

Chapter Four: The Gang of Four

Flying from London Heathrow to Kalamata via Thomas Cook Airlines the next day were our four cats: Spankie, Marley, Gibson and Franklin.

As is often the case with cats, the original name that you give them evolves over time, so for these, and all of the subsequent cats, I will include their alter egos.

Spankie *(Spankington, Spanks, Spankie Pants, Fatty Spanks)*

Spankie was my first cat, adopted from a rescue shelter in 2002. I had bought my first flat in London before meeting Anne and was desperate to have animals. As the house had a large, long, secure garden it was perfect for cats and due to the long hours I was working back then a dog just wasn't feasible. Spanks was her own cat, and she didn't like me very much. On the very first day I adopted her she bit me and things didn't get a lot better with time. She also bit Anne on the first day they met. But that was fine, I loved the company and after a week of two of getting to know each other we settled into an easy routine: she demanded something, I gave it to her.

She was a very pretty long haired tabby. The shelter told me that she had been found in a burned out building, left by the previous owners. I was worried about the length of her hair - and that of the other three - in the Greek heat, but I needn't have worried as it turned out they loved the heat.

I got **Marley** *(Marls, Raymondo, Marlington, Marley-moos, Marley Stanfield)* about a year after Spankie, from Archway Cat Rescue, North London.

She was a long haired black cat with the most amazing eyes. Also a bit of a loner, she didn't have much of a back story other than she had been adopted a week before I got her, but brought back 'because she slept all day'. Seriously. Yes, so the name is a little bit obvious, but in my defence it was a few years before the eponymous book/film about the dog of the same name and there was some history there.

I am obsessed by music, as is Anne, and love Bob Marley. Back when I was very young my father worked at Island Records, installing their very first computer system. He used to have to work at nights and he would come home in the morning to wake me up before primary school and tell me all these stories about some guys from Jamaica recording for Island. At the time he left out the story about the amazing herbal aroma that followed them around, but I do remember him telling me how impressed he was that these chaps from Trenchtown, a Jamaican slum, could all write sheet music, something no one that he knew could do. I was later told by a friend that while recording they ordered in a barrel of Jamaican sea water as they didn't like washing their dreadlocks in British water and apparently Island Records' boss, Chris Blackwell, who had signed them, agreed to foot the bill.

Two years hence, Marley would have the use of a three bedroom house overlooking the Mediterranean all to herself, but that is a story for later. She would treat our place like a teenager - come in for food and then just leave. She was semi-feral, but in the first six months of Greece she turned almost completely feral, like a kid in a sweet shop.

Any guitar player - like me - will tell you that one of the finest guitars one can play is a **Gibson**, so that was the name of the third 'original' *(Gibbo, Gibsonio, Gorgeous Gibs, Princess)*.

Gibson is a tabby Maine Coon with a magnificent tail and the first cat that Anne and I got together. She is scared of her own shadow, scared of cat flaps, scared of most things - bless her - but she is the most beautiful, loving cat that one could wish for. She has a habit of sleeping on Anne's pillow, something we call 'Gibbo Pillow'. We adore her.

The last 'original' was Gibson's half sister, **Franklin** *(Frankie, Frankie Bear, Renegade Franklin, MC Ren)*, a tortoiseshell Maine Coon.

Continuing with the musical theme - a theme that runs through this whole book - she is named after my musical hero, Adam Franklin, singer and guitarist for 90s band, Swervedriver. As you might have probably guessed by now, we didn't really mind giving female cats male names and vice versa. Also, we had forgone our right to criticise any name given to animal or child as 'silly'.

Swervedriver are the best band you have never heard of - well, in my view anyway. They were signed to Creation records, home of Oasis, when Creation boss Alan McGee heard their demo tape while somewhat chemically enhanced in a limousine in LA. Then Britpop happened and they were criminally forgotten in the UK, whilst still big in the US.

They reformed in 2008, a couple of years before this book starts, and Anne promised me we could go to their first show, thinking it would probably be a London one. I was overjoyed to see that the first show was the Henry Fonda Theatre, Los Angeles, and Anne was good as her word. We hired a Ford Mustang and a Harley Davidson and stayed in a pool bungalow at the Chateau Marmont, where the actor Dustin Hoffman was our neighbour.

One day by the pool, Anne spotted someone walking towards us and nudged me - it was Reservoir Dogs star Tim Roth. I didn't have my glasses on and replied under my breath 'No way, I can't believe we're staying in the same hotel as … *Bryan Adams*'.

Anyway, Franklin was my favourite cat, I adored her. I adore all my cats and I'm not sure one should even have a favourite, but there it is, I've said it. She was incredibly affectionate and would follow you around miaowing, demanding tummy rubs. For some strange reason she adored the heavy rain, so frequently I would be asleep in bed with a storm raging outside and be awoken by 5kg of soaking Maine Coon on my head. She was just *so* proud of herself.

Chapter Five: Stoupa, Baby!

We had no mobile phone reception on the ferry, but as we passed our beloved Kefalonia, where our love affair with Greece started, Anne began to get messages on her phone. From the look on her face, all was not well. The company we were using to transport the cats had called to say that at the last minute Thomas Cook had changed the plane that they were using to fly to Kalamata to one with no cargo hold for animals. Rather unhelpfully they had offered us another flight in three weeks' time. Anne was in tears. We had torn through Europe at a crazy pace to be here in time for the flight to land and the cats wouldn't be on it.

We were so upset and angry, but we had little choice other than to continue on to Stoupa while our agents handled the mess and tried to get the cats onto another, earlier flight. According to the small print Thomas Cook could pretty much do as they liked, so we were helpless. What a way to start our new life - no cats and a wife in tears.

The drive from Patras to Stoupa took us five hours, filled with curses and vague plans of revenge. Nine years later, of course, Thomas Cook would collapse into administration. Don't mess with us!

May 1st 2010: May Day in Greece. It is always a fantastic, fun day in Stoupa, where the village celebrates the start of summer and the tourist season, as it was back then, as the first package flights would land in the final days of April. There are flowers everywhere, on tavernas, on car windows underneath windscreen wipers, on house doors. It almost felt as if the village had come out to welcome us. After a very quick drink with our new landlord at his taverna, we set off on the ten minute drive up the mountain to our new home: a two bedroom, three floor Mani Tower set well away from other houses, with enough land to grow all the vegetables we wanted and with olive groves out in front of us for as far as the eye could see until the Mediterranean. We were just at the top end of walking distance to Stoupa, but it felt like we were in the middle of nowhere.

I still vividly remember walking up the steps to the front door for the first time. This was it, our new home for the next two years!

That evening we had steak and chips with wine on the terrace admiring our new view.

I've touched on Stoupa before, but it really is a hidden gem.

Kalogria Bay

Stoupa Bay

With the Taygetos Mountains lurking behind it, Stoupa is a small village in mainland South West Greece, approximately an hour from its nearest city and airport of Kalamata. It is centred around three beaches, each with their own unique charms. Its year round population is most probably well under 1000, but that number increases rapidly once the good weather and the tourist season comes.

Ah yes, the weather. Stoupa is located in an area known as The Mani, itself part of The Peloponnese, which is mainland Greece, but also technically an island as the Corinth Canal cuts it off from Athens and the North. The easiest way to see where it is on a map is to look at Greece and then look at the bottom of the mainland (Peloponnese). There are three fingers and Stoupa is situated half way down the West coast of the middle finger.

The Mani is sometimes referred to as 'The California of Greece' due to its fantastic weather. Its latitude is the same as Tunisia in North Africa, so summers are hot - sometimes uncomfortably hot - and winters are generally short and mild.

Winter is December to the end of February, with the start of the season often bright and sunny, sometimes 20^0C or above, and February normally very wet and often incredibly windy and can get quite chilly. Spring starts in March and by mid-April it is normally comfortably over 25^0C most days. Due to cold mountain water run-off I usually delay swimming in the sea until May, but many people swim all year round. Alongside February, August is the most uncomfortable month and temperatures can reach 50^0C, with the sand on the beach too hot to casually stroll over. We call it 'monkey sand' as you can't walk on it without involuntarily going 'ooh ooh, aah aah'. By September it is common for there to have been little or no rain for five months.

Around its beaches Stoupa has approximately 30 tavernas or bars, with further places to eat and drink in neighbouring villages.

I always tell my friends that if they want glitz and glamour, five star luxury and Michelin starred restaurants (with the corresponding prices) to go to Mykonos and not here. But if you want gorgeous sandy beaches, a beautifully relaxed atmosphere, to read a book on the beach, swim in turquoise waters, dry off and walk into a taverna in your swimming gear for a cold beer at €2.50 then this is the place for you.

Stoupa is becoming well known now, but really only became a 'resort' in the early 1990s, when flights began to land at Kalamata airport, which was previously only used by the military. Perhaps you remember the British plane spotters who got arrested and jailed, charged with espionage around the turn of the century? They were acquitted finally, but their 'crimes' took place at Kalamata airport. It seemed that 'plane spotting' isn't a 'thing' in Greece.

Before tourism came, olives were the main source of income. Stoupa itself is relatively new, as the Maniots tended to live further up the mountain due to raids by pirates. There are some that claim true Maniots are descended from pirates and from what I can gather there is at least some truth in this. Certainly, the Maniots have a fearsome reputation as warriors. Indeed the revolution to throw out the Turkish occupiers in 1821 started just down the road in Limeni Bay, led by local warlord Mavromichalis ('Black Mike').

(L) Anne blowing the seeds off a dandelion at the north end of Stoupa Bay

The main village has three beaches: Kalogria, the main Stoupa bay and Halikoura. Kalogria is perhaps the most beautiful beach in Southern mainland Greece, huge expanses of sand, gently sloping with a number of fine tavernas and bars on its fringe. It also has a rather interesting natural phenomenon, which is unique in Greece, a source of fresh water from the Taygetos Mountains behind the village manifesting itself in fresh water springs in a number of different places in the sea, so at one point you are swimming in lovely warm Mediterranean water and then the next you are hit by icy fresh water. There is a rock pool, called The Pritzipas - named after a wonderful taverna next to it - that is exclusively fed by a mountain spring which stays at 11 degrees all year round. It is wonderful to cool off in, but I've never managed more than 30 seconds fully submerged before leaping out, freezing.

Just behind the rock pool is a small, unassuming, whitewashed stone house. In around 1917 its inhabitant was Nikos Kazantzakis, a famous Greek author, who at the time worked in a lignite mine just outside the village. He had a fun friend also living with him, a real character. During the day they would work in the mine and in the evening they would swim, dance, relax and cook food on Kalogria beach.

The lignite mine closed down and Kazantzakis wrote a book with his friend as the central character. His friend's name was Zorba, and although both the book and film, Zorba the Greek, were set in Crete their origins lie in Stoupa. There is a statue of Kazantzakis overlooking Kalogria and also a huge mural of him to celebrate this part of the village's history.

OK ... Stick with me on this bit because initially it might seem to be completely unrelated and we also need to go back over 30 years. I was 16, music mad and had very relaxed parents. Together with two best mates I would travel from Reading to London up to two or three times a week to see our favourite bands. Fake IDs meant we could have a few drinks and by the time we got back to Reading our hunger was growing. If we made it back before midnight there was a white kebab van parked in a bus stop opposite the train station. We would always go for the same thing - large doner kebab, loads of vegetables, extra hot chili sauce, with the finest cuts of meat from the spinning stick.

The kebab van was called Zorba's. In the space of 30 years I had gone from underage drinking at gigs and eating doner kebabs from Mr Zorba in Reading, to living a few kilometres from the actual beach where Zorba himself lived - full circle in a funny kind of way.

The other side of the Taygetos Mountains is the city of Sparta, in the district of Lakonia.

The Greeks are well-known for one word answers in letters, the most famous being a one word response to the Germans in WW2 who demanded to be able to invade peacefully - '*Oxi*', or 'no'. Oxi Day is now a national holiday.

Many years ago the Spartans were sent a letter from the Macedonians saying that they were going to invade and 'if we successfully invade, we will'... followed by a series of threats.

The Spartans replied with just one word: 'if'. The Lakonia region then became the source of the word 'laconic', meaning to converse with few words.

Chapter Six: Year One, 2010, Settling In.

Our immediate tasks on our first full day in the new home were four-fold: arrange for the cats to get out here as soon as possible, clean the house, get the garden ready for planting vegetables, and wait for the shipment of our belongings to arrive.

The cats were pretty much out of our hands, although we missed them and wanted them here as soon as possible.   This is the advantage of employing agents to transport animals - they know the airlines, the schedules, which planes carry animal cargo and which don't. More importantly than that, they had something we didn't: a phone line.

It was decided that I would do the garden and Anne clean the house. This wasn't just some sexist division of labour as you will see later in the book. We divide the jobs up equally according to who is best suited to the task, so for example I do almost all the cooking and stack the dishwasher, while Anne grapples with all the electrical and IT issues.

But it is fair to say though that I got the best job this time. Both tasks were arduous and backbreaking in the 80-90 degree heat, but at least I was outside ridding myself of my pasty white English winter colouring, while poor Anne was scrubbing toilets and up to her elbows in bleach, not getting any sun at all. We toiled for a week and by the end of that we had a sparkling house ready for all our furniture, books, guitars etc. We also had a cleared garden with a hammock and about ten beds dug out for planting vegetables.

This was our first mistake in a long list of mistakes that we made. Later on I will go into far more depth about growing fruit and vegetables in Greece, tips we have learned errors made. I have also compiled a list of general mistakes that people make when moving to Greece. The vast majority of those were also made by us and I would hate for others to experience the stress and sometimes the cost and heartache that they entailed. Once is enough.

Mid-May is *way* too late to start growing vegetables in Greece. It really is almost too late to even plant the seedlings you can buy in the garden centres here. Once you get into June, temperatures really start to rise, by July and August you are in the kind of territory where new, unestablished plants just wither and die. Hardly anything I can think of is planted or grown in those months other than some long established tomatoes, courgettes and a few other plants in shady areas, yet they are the very months that UK gardeners love. You really do need to rip up the UK gardening rule book for so many reasons.

That's not to say that the digging that I did, which caused a recurrence of an old tennis elbow injury, was a waste. I could use them from mid-September onwards, just not now. We had to be content with a few salad leaves grown in the shade for the time being.

We did take the occasional break in our first week, popping down to the bay for a swim and lunch in a taverna.

It showed us that despite having a two year lease on a Greek house, we were still very much in a London state of mind.

Firstly, walking along the seafront there were maybe ten scooters parked, all with keys in the ignition and helmets just resting on the seat, no locks whatsoever. We couldn't believe it. As I mentioned earlier, back in London we both owned Vespas and despite thick chains and locks they would regularly be stolen, the below-seat compartment broken into or just vandalised. Once, we found that someone had cut both fuel lines to siphon out the petrol. The most fuel I had ever put into the tank was about £6, and neither bike was full, so for what cost us £200 to fix they might have made away with a maximum of £10 of petrol. What a low budget, low ambition thief!

To see the bikes on Stoupa seafront just left unattended with the keys in etc was astounding. That's not to say that crime doesn't occur here, as I will sadly write about later, it is just that it is not as widespread and in fact it is very, very rare; newsworthy even.

The second reminder that we were still in a London state of mind came just five metres later on our walk. Anne pointed out that a part of the beach had been cordoned off with tape - 'Do you think there has been a murder!?' Murders were not yet that common in our part of London when we left, although gang-related crime did spill over and we did have a drive-by shooting a few hundred yards from our house just the week before leaving for Greece. Sadly, in the years after we left there was a huge surge in gang-related murder in London, mainly knife crime.

We got closer and saw a sign: 'CARETTA-CARETTA': turtles! Eggs had been laid and a local had noticed and sealed off the area where they were. I later learned this was important as if just one stray beach lounger or parasol pole broke an egg it could infect the rest of the eggs and mean that no turtles at all hatched.

We got back to be informed by our landlord that OTE, the Greek phone company were ready to come tomorrow to install our phone line and broadband the next day, just as promised. Whereas UK telecoms companies have a somewhat poor reputation, OTE, now known as COSMOTE, have always been brilliant for us, although we are aware that not all our neighbours share our view, having had differing levels of service to us.

This week had been blissful ignorance on our part, despite the fact that we knew a General Election was happening in the UK. We hadn't read a paper or the internet, nor spoken to anybody. Once the work was carried out we tested out our broadband and discovered that the UK was in somewhat of a stasis: no overall majority had been won by a single party and Gordon Brown didn't seem to want to leave Number 10.

Of far more importance and interest to me was the fact that our new broadband was amazingly fast, indeed better than we had previously in London. How could that be? We were half the way up a mountain in rural Greece in a house that didn't even have an address!

We even had a brand new, very easy to remember telephone number, ending in 64000. Who couldn't remember the $64,000 question?

That night I was awoken at around 2am by the phone ringing and a confused Greek man on the line. I hadn't yet learned any Greek and he hung up on me after repeating a word to me that I didn't understand. This happened the next night, and the next and became a regular occurrence during the week, with callers saying a now familiar word repeatedly.

In the end I wrote the word down phonetically and asked a friendly neighbour what it could mean.

'Nosso-kom-eyo'

She laughed and did a quick internet search. Sure enough, the local hospital - *'nosokomeio'* - in Kalamata (by 'local' I mean an hour's drive away on treacherous mountain roads) had almost exactly the same number - 46000 instead of our 64000. Great.

This would continue to bug us until we had the number changed, but it did result in a 'first' for us in Greece: my friend taught us our first Greek phrase and numbers. We realised that a lot of the people were quite frightened when ringing - who rings a hospital for a polite chat? - so we decided to learn how to tell them that they had the wrong number and to be able to give them the correct one instead. It worked most of the time, but there were still a number of people who were most put out that at 2am in the morning they had incorrectly dialled and woken up an Englishman with limited Greek, resulting in the phone being slammed down on me.

We heard that our London possessions were going to be delivered, which soon led us to ask three questions that had been troubling us:

1. How do you deliver a truck of belongings to a house with no address?

2. How do you get a van into a small hamlet that has a low brick archway at its entrance?

3. How do you get a van along a very narrow 100 ft driveway?

The answer to the first question was simpler than we thought: they drove to our landlord's taverna, his son jumped on his dirt bike and told them to follow him for the 3km it took to get to our house. He took them by a rocky, unmade road to avoid the brick archway. But how do you get a large truck down a narrow, 100ft driveway? Answer: You don't, you just dump the entire load at the end of the drive and leave them there on a day when it was over 90 degrees.

I forget how many times I drove and then reversed my car along that track in the heat that day - maybe 20? - but it was too many, especially when the joy of assembling beds, wardrobes and shelves awaited.

The agents dealing with the transportation of the cats contacted us and had managed to get the cats on a BA flight to Athens for the next day. At the time, a motorway was in the final stages of construction between Athens and Kalamata, which means you can now make the journey in three and a half hours, but when we had to drive to pick up the cats, the drive to Athens from Stoupa would take five and a half hours. We planned to do the round trip in one go, so 11 hours of driving, plus however many hours of waiting. Stupidly we took directions from our satnav, an out of date satnav as it turned out, that took us along the *old* Athens road. In places it was virtually a dirt road, but the satnav kept telling us that we were nearly at the end and joining a new road. We believed it the first time, gave it the benefit of the doubt the second time and by the third time we were too far along to turn back.

We were so nervous about the safety of the cats, worried that we would be late - you name it, we were nervous about it - so we left home super early, but even after this awful and long detour we still arrived hours before the flight. Right opposite Athens Airport is an IKEA, so we decided to pop in for a cup of tea and cheesecake. Did I mention that we were nervous? Anne couldn't even eat her cheesecake. This. Never. Happens.

At the time the flight was due to land, we left IKEA, crossed over the motorway and pulled up at the cargo bays. A small amount of paperwork later we were told to head to 'Bay One' and drove straight there, to find a pallet with three cat boxes on top. The cats had arrived, safe and sound, at last! We gave them all a hug, but, conscious of time, set off for home fairly swiftly.

Gibson and Franklin, the two Maine Coon sisters were together in one cat box. Both were fairly distressed and it was heart breaking to see Franklin, the younger sister, comforting Gibson. Spankie and Marley had their own boxes, given that they really didn't like one another, or indeed anyone else. They sat in their boxes in the back of the car, no doubt plotting our slow and painful deaths for putting them through all of this, while Gibson cried out every 30 seconds for the entire five and a half hours back. We finally made it home at 2am, let the cats out in their new home and headed to bed.

Within about five minutes, Gibson was pacing up and down the spiral staircase, obviously very confused, making lots of noise. This continued until the morning.

Up earlier than planned, we opened the terrace and gave the cats their first view of their new garden.

Gibson's first taste of Greek freedom!

I am conscious that recommended advice is to keep cats in a new home for a week, but in reality with ours it was just not going to happen. They were all desperate to be outside and so after a couple of days of frustration, both for them and for us, we let them out.

Some people judge success by their salary, job, house, wife, kids etc. I said before we moved to Greece that we would have succeeded when we saw our cats running through an olive grove. Watching them run off into the grove in front of our house was just a wonderful, wonderful feeling.

Finally, the family was all together again.

Summer was hotting up and I started wearing a combination of clothes that I would continue to wear: shorts of some variety, t-shirt (optional), beads and flip flops. This would continue even throughout winter with an added hoodie. Even when I went back to the UK I would wear flip flops, as shoes just didn't feel right any more. In the past decade I can count on my fingers the number of times I have worn shoes, mostly for weddings and funerals. My winter attire used to really annoy Anne, who insisted I put shoes on when it was cold and rainy, but I told her repeatedly that as I live in the Mediterranean there was no need. I have stuck by that rather stubborn mantra to this day, even when it is really cold.

We took June and July easy, then the brutal heat of August hit. I remember being at times elated that we had made the move, but also being somewhat down, worried that maybe it would end and we would have to go back to the UK.

Around the middle of August we came back from a day at the beach to find a message from my mother. She had cancer; bowel cancer. The news knocked me sideways. It is hard enough getting that sort of news in the first place, but not being able to hug her - and Dad who was taking it particularly badly - was heart-breaking. Everything seemed so far away right then.

Up until that point in life I had been lucky - *The Big C, AKA 'The Sod'*, hadn't featured in my life. I was blissfully ignorant about terminology, survival rates and types of treatment. Sadly, this was the start of a steep and painful learning process on several fronts over many years.

I learned that there were four stages of cancer and was hopeful that Mum's cancer, caught early, could be treated. She had just gone to a doctor on an unrelated matter and mentioned as an aside that she was feeling breathless. I believe that doctors are warned that this is an early sign, something I never knew. As I said, this was a learning curve, a steep and painful one. I was also told that quite often the partner of a cancer sufferer must be looked after almost as much as the patient and this would become the case as the months passed. My parents had been together since the age of 13, almost 50 years, and this hit Dad especially hard.

I don't know if something got lost in translation, but I spoke to Mum's oncologist for over an hour on the phone, trying to understand exactly what the future held. She was very reluctant to give out statistics on survival, but when pushed said that this was stage 4 cancer - of four. WHAT!? Mum would be recommended a course of treatment that included an operation to remove the tumours and a severe dose of chemotherapy. The oncologist described this as 'the big guns', where you try and obliterate the cancer, rather than the chemotherapy that slows down the growth in the tumours to prolong life. In the end she told me that Mum had a 15% chance of seeing 2014.

Still trying to process the information, I decided that a stiff drink was in order, so we drove down to the supermarket to buy some wine. It was there that we saw our first example of just how poor Greek driving is, although we would be constantly reminded of it throughout our first decade.

As I hope will become evident as you read this book, I adore the Greek people with a passion. I love their sense of rebellion, their laidback attitude, their celebration of outdoor life with good food, wine and dancing late into the night. This, however, does not exclude me from commenting on a few of the bad sides of Greece and Greek people ... and their driving sits firmly at the top of that list.

I often wonder if the Greek driving test includes a section where you have to drive with a coffee in one hand and a cigarette in the other, or perhaps maybe a parallel parking exercise while texting.

In the UK I had a rule that rarely had exceptions: the worst drivers were male, old and owned a Nissan Micra. A friend's grandfather once complained about 'that absolute idiot who designed the motorways, making the driver in the really slow lane have to come off at every junction'. It soon dawned on us that he had been driving down the hard shoulder. He had a Nissan Micra. See?

Old ✓

Male ✓

Micra Driver✓

As we drove to the supermarket we saw an erratically driven Micra in front of us, old man at the wheel. He was all over the shop, both lanes at times, braking unnecessarily, a total danger to other road users. I very carefully overtook and shouted '*malaka!*' at him, once again, still in a London frame of mind. My rage turned to absolute shock when I saw his face: it was a Greek Orthodox priest.

Ticket Seller: 'Where would you like to go please?'

Me: 'Hell'.

Ticket Seller: 'Is that a return or a single?'

Me; 'A single will do, thanks'.

The year ended with Greece still in a perilous state politically and economically. What had 'just' been a banking crisis soon took hold and became a sovereign crisis. On the Greek side there was a mountain of debt that could never realistically be paid back, so a debt forgiveness programme or 'haircut' was needed. On the EU side, led by the Germans, no German politician could write off Greek debt without facing being voted out. It was stalemate. Austerity was implemented/enforced and in one week during the austerity debate we had regular power cuts at odd times in protest. A camping stove kept us in tea and hot meals and was worth its weight in gold.

Anne and I celebrated our first wedding anniversary with drinks and then dinner on the flat roof of our Mani tower, looking at the view through the 'turrets'. For Christmas we started a now annual tradition of cooking a huge turkey, going for a very bracing dip in the sea and then coming back on Boxing Day to feed all of the turkey off-cuts - 'stiggy bits' as I used to call them as a child - to the stray cat crew on the beach in Stoupa Bay.

Oh, hang on. Something else important happened that year too ...

Chapter Seven: Our First Greek Cat, Jeeves

We had 'The Four Originals' and had no intention of getting any more cats. They were nicely settled in their new home country and besides, with the economic situation as it was, we wanted to be able to throw all of our possessions into the car, cats included, and drive out of Greece should the situation require it. I never kept the car less than three quarters full of petrol and four cats would be our absolute limit for a long drive. In addition, we only had permission for four cats from our landlord.

Our Mani Tower backed onto a complex of lovely stone holiday homes, run by a German chap called Johann.

There was an on-site taverna and we ate there regularly as it was just a short walk from ours. One meal in June we found ourselves at a table there with two black and white kittens scrounging for food, a very common occurrence in Greece. We fed them pieces of pork fillet and steak from our meal and thought nothing more of it.

Those cats congregated by the communal bins - another very common Greek occurrence - but while the holiday makers were about they lived the good life. However, come October the holiday makers had gone home and pickings were slim.

Anne and I were watching TV one evening in mid-October when we heard a scratch on the door and a 'miaow'. We opened the door to find the same black and white kitten we had fed a few months previously. We gave him some treats, then he ended up on my lap and, well, he obviously hadn't read the 'no more cats' memo, so he decided to move in. Even if we had held firm it just wouldn't have worked; he had decided.

His markings were quite unique, it almost looked like he had a bow tie on his neck, or a bit like the character that you see on the side of tubes of Pringles. Moving away from our habit of naming cats on musical related themes, we thought he looked like a butler, so we named him Jeeves, although that name would mutate many times over the years.

Jeeves (Jeevsey Shitbag, The Taliban, Mr Pringle, Jeeves-os)

Had we known the grief he would cause us over the years we probably might have thought twice about taking him in. He has caused us more trouble than all of our other cats combined. Jeeves is a fighter and now only has two front teeth left as the rest had to be taken out by our vet on separate occasions as they had snapped off while fighting. He fought with our other cats, Gibson in particular. When we moved to our second house he attacked the neighbours' cats, which of course doesn't make you popular, especially when we later moved to a little hamlet further up the mountain named Marmoutsa. We later learned that the neighbours called him 'The Taliban' and he caused us and them no end of distress. We were responsible cat owners, neutering, chipping and vaccinating every cat we owned and the thought of him causing harm to other animals - and our own - mortified us.

But he was only an alpha male 2% of the time. The rest of the time he was the most amazing, cuddly lap cat, always on the bed to provide winter warmth. We later spotted that he was worse around full moon, and he had a particular walk, *a 'pimp roll'*, that would signal that he was about to be up to no good.

Should I admit this next bit? Well, in for a penny, in for a pound.

Jeeves continued in the tradition of all of our cats having songs written about them. He had a fair number written, but perhaps the most memorable was [to 'Jenny from the Block' by Jennifer Lopez].

'Don't be fooled by my rocks and my bling

I'm still, I'm still Jeevesey from the bins'

Hmmm, that might not make the final edit, but for now it stays.

Chapter Eight: Year 2, 2011, Time to Move On?

We had signed a two year lease on the Mani Tower, taking us up to 1st May 2012. Although we loved the house and its positioning, it was beginning to become clear that it was not for us long term.

The kitchen was tiny, more akin to one you would find in a holiday home, and this led to a few what Anne would call 'kitchen diva strops' from me while cooking. The staircases in the house were metal and spiral and could be lethal if you slipped. More importantly, there was no heating, open fire or log burner, and after a very cold Greek winter it was clear that these were 'must haves' - our soaring electricity bill from halogen heaters could attest to this.

The winter was so cold that we ended up sleeping in hooded tops, Anne stealing my favourite red one and doing the hood up so tight that she looked like Kenny from South Park.

There was one further major problem - the flat roof, which leaked. We ended up with a green ceiling, being mould from water ingress, and together with the cold air, it wasn't a good mix for your health and comfort. The window ledges unbelievably sloped inwards, meaning any rain was trapped there and ultimately found its way through into the house.

We decided to look around for a new house to rent. In the UK it is pretty easy, although we all have either heard of or experienced horror stories of unscrupulous letting agents charging excess fees etc - I know I have. At the time there were only two 'proper' agencies, with the rest of the houses mainly for sale by builders, taverna owners or anyone else who is open to offers. But given the Greek crisis, nothing was selling, meaning a number of houses were available to rent.

Whilst people in the UK often moan about the clichéd fat-tied estate agents in branded Mini Coopers, I almost missed them. Much of the rental process here is done by word of mouth and that meant you avoided the 10% fee on the first year's rent that the local agents charged the tenant, but it wasn't a simple process by any means. An agent charging a tenant was a new concept to me particularly as they were also charging the landlord - nice lucrative business if you can get it.

One day Anne spotted a gorgeous house for sale on an independent website, no agents involved. We discussed it and as both of us are of the view that 'if you don't ask you don't get', she sent off an email to the vendors asking if they might consider renting rather than selling. They responded positively and we arranged to meet, with them flying over from the UK.

It wasn't until January 2012 that we even saw the inside of the house in person, but for now we were in love with the place. Most importantly we had been informed that there were absolutely no busy roads anywhere nearby. Does anyone else choose their house with their cats as the number one priority?

Given the continuing economic crisis, the Greek government decided to implement a property tax. I forget the exact amount that it was for our house as the landlord had to pay it, but it was approximately €700 per annum. To avoid evasion it was issued as part of the electricity bill - if you don't pay, you don't have electricity. The amount was calculated referencing the age of the house, its location and its size in square metres. The Church, one of the richest organisations in Greece and the owner of thousands of properties, was exempt.

My friend rented a house, one of two owned by the same landlord, and was surprised one day to find an official at his door. The official pointed out that the landlord had taken an electricity feed from my friend's house to supply his other house, therefore only having to pay one property tax rather than two.

In Greece, a pool is counted as part of your property, meaning if you have a large pool you pay a larger property tax. Many are not declared. One well-heeled suburb of Athens had just a few hundred pools according to official records, but when Greek officials took aerial photographs they identified more than 20,000 pools. Word spread quickly and all the local available AstroTurf supplies were

bought up to put on as pool covers to thwart aerial surveillance.
'Where there is a bill there is a will'.

Moving to Greece was such a quick decision that we hadn't had the
chance to learn any of the language, beyond helping people to
understand that our Mani Tower was not, in fact, Kalamata Hospital.
We decided to start Greek lessons with a wonderful, patient lady at a
school overlooking the beach. Ten years on and we can both speak
and write the language, enough to get by and chat, but not 100%
fluent.

Both Anne and I spoke fluent French, indeed at my last job the main
spoken language was French - at a German owned company in
London. My colleagues came from as far as Guadeloupe, but mostly
Paris, Belgium or Luxembourg. French had come easily and I studied
it at university alongside economics. But Greek? Greek was
something else altogether. It is not just that the alphabet was
different. Anyone who has studied maths beyond GCSE would
recognise most of the letters, although some were deliberately tricky,
as they looked just like English letters, yet meant something altogether
different. For example, one of my favourite words in Greek is
'TAVERNA', for obvious reasons. That in Greek is 'TABEPNA'.

There are 18 ways of saying 'the'. All numbers are neutral, other than
three and four, which are feminine. Yes, it was hard, but our lovely
teacher kept us going when we started feeling down about it. I often
felt that we would really have a breakthrough at times, only for the
next week to be completely flummoxed by some new grammar or
discovering there are also 18 ways to say 'a/an'!

I was told that other than Japanese, Greek is the hardest language in
the world to learn. Apparently Japanese is spoken at seven different

levels of complexity and some Japanese don't even reach level seven. Being of the stubborn persuasion, this really spurred me on. I *will* succeed. (I later found out that Greek isn't even in the top ten hardest languages to learn, but that didn't matter for now).

I think Anne found it annoying to learn Greek with me. In fact, I *know* Anne found it annoying to learn with me, as I generally left homework to the last minute and this wound her up no end as she likes to get her homework done straight away. I justified this somewhat lax attitude to study by saying that if I did the homework at the last minute it would still be fresh in my head for the lesson.

We would continue these weekly classes for three more years.

If I had to give five tips on learning the language they would be:

1. **Get Lessons:** The alphabet is different, deceptive to an English speaker at times and at a bare minimum you should get lessons to teach you this, how to read, numbers, days of the week and simple phrases; point you in the right direction. I would suggest a 30 minute lesson a week, plus homework. I took lessons in the off season, so October to April.

2. **Always Speak Greek When Out:** Most Greeks, especially the younger Greeks, speak English and it is easy to lapse into just speaking your mother tongue. When ordering food or drinks, or in a shop, speak Greek and if they answer in English, reply back in Greek. Take every opportunity to practise.

3. **At Lessons Ask Things Relevant to You:** We had to pick up a package from the Post Office and I knew the man then working there didn't speak English. Our teacher supplied the phrases to use and I have never forgotten them. Similarly, our wonderful teacher took us through our electricity bill, explaining each part. We learned how to explain where to find our house, since there are very few addresses here. Learning phrases that you know you need, then using them in daily life helps it stick.

4. **Persevere:** Sometimes you feel like you are making some headway, and then something new comes and completely floors you. It *is* hard, and Greeks know how hard it is. Unlike in perhaps some other European countries, I have never heard of a Greek correcting your grammar; I think they are genuinely happy that you are at least trying to learn the language. I quickly learned how to say 'I am sorry, I am trying to learn Greek' (*'signomi, prostatho na matheno Ellinika)'* and the inevitable answer is *'siga, siga'* or *'slowly, slowly'* nearly always accompanied by a smile.

5. **Learn From Your Mistakes:** My eldest niece is called Georgia, which is a popular name in Greece, pronounced *'Yee-orr-yee-a'*. It also means 'agriculture' in Greek and I have absolutely no idea how I know that, it probably came from an exercise I did at school - one exercise invariably leads to several more.

My family were coming over and so I asked our teacher to spend the lesson teaching me how to introduce my family, so 'This is my father/brother, he lives in the UK/Switzerland' etc. From that I had to learn all the familial vocabulary like mother, father, brother etc plus then it led to a lesson on countries of the world.

I had been testing my nascent Greek out whenever I could and, not unlike in the TV series Alan Partridge where the main character only had 'friends' at the Travelodge where he lived, my only real 'friends' were people that worked in the local supermarket.

There was a lovely lady there in her 30s who I would chat to and so I asked what her name was and she said Georgia. I then said 'my niece is called Georgia! She is coming to Stoupa in two weeks'

The next time I was in the supermarket I walked in all cocky and saw her, so I shouted out 'Kalimera Yia-yia', being careful to get the pronunciation precisely correct. She was distinctly cold with me when I was at the checkout. I thought this odd and told my Greek teacher at the next lesson and she asked me to repeat what I had said. It was then that all became clear.

Instead of calling her '*Yee-orr-yee-a*' ('Georgia') I had called her 'Yia-yia' ('Grandma').

That is how I learned to say 'I am very sorry, I have made a mistake' in Greek. As I said, one exercise invariably leads to several more.

Once things had calmed down and cooled down I got the chance to use the planting beds I had dug out in the May/June heat the previous year. We grew peas, courgettes, salad, peppers, tomatoes, spinach, potatoes, spring onions and managed some really decent crops. At one time the courgettes were so plentiful that we had 18 bags of curried courgette soup in the freezer.

Much as I hated it as a task, I was still tolerating strimming the garden on our small-ish plot and one day spotted something out of the corner of my eye - this lovely chap, about the size of a €2 coin.

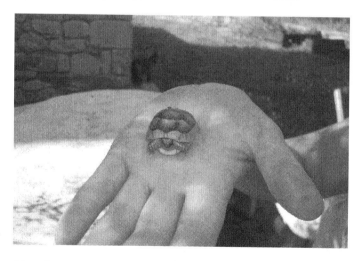

We said at the start of the year 'no more cats' and managed to stick to this rule … for this year at least.

Chapter Nine: 2012, A New House

We had a tentative agreement to rent a new house, yet had only seen photos of it. From the photos we managed to guess roughly where the house was located and one day we decided to set out and find it. I remember that day well - it was my 38th birthday.

We narrowed it down to three roads just outside of the old village of Neochori (*'New Town'*) and set out to explore. It turned out to be on a road known locally - most likely named by estate agents - as 'The Neochori Balcony' in Marmoutsa, so named because there is a sheer drop below and no one can build in front of it due to the gorge. I had grown used to these fancy names that estate agents invent to describe areas from my time in North London. Archway had been called 'Highgate Slopes' and a particular part of Archway that my friends lived in was renamed 'Whitehall Park Conservation Area'. I have also heard stories that Streatham was renamed 'St. Reatham', but surely that's not true, is it?

As we drove down the dead end concrete road I got more and more excited. We passed a large field and then on the right, with 180 degree unimpeded views of the Mediterranean, there it was. *Oh my.* It was a three storey house made from Taygetos stone, the mountains that rose up behind the house. There was a large carport with wooden structure to cover the car. Bougainvillea and other exotic flowered vines entwined the structure to provide total cover. In front of the house was a formal garden with rosemary, orange and lemon trees, fig trees, grapevines and wild almond trees. To the far side of the house was a field of approximately 1,000m^2 with rocky outcrops, a few oak trees and wild sage and thyme. At the end of the field was an enchanting secret garden, hidden below a large rock overhang.

To the left as you looked at the sea there were majestic mountain peaks that would get a covering of snow in later winters and up to four - four! - peninsulas in sight on a good day. Right below was the gorgeous fishing village and harbour of Agios Nikolaos (Saint Nicholas) with its fishing boats leaving behind a delicate wake in the sea as they left before the sun came up. At 45 degrees to the right in the far distance was the end of the bay the first of three fingers of the Peloponnese, the village of Finikounda, with an island just south that was once used as target practice by the Greek Air Force. And to the far right, on our middle peninsula, over the brow of a hill, was Stoupa.

I was in love with the house and I hadn't even seen inside!

We had a walk around the garden and the field and I was just elated. This was a place where the cats would be totally safe, far from busy roads, with just a handful of houses nearby, perfect for us to keep ourselves to ourselves. The fact that we saw one of the neighbours and he had a cat tattoo on his shoulder told us it was meant to be. You know how sometimes in life you just *know*? We had to secure this.

We drove back down the mountain to our place which had served us incredibly well through our first 20 months in Greece, but now just didn't seem to compare.

Me: *'Oh my God, oh my God, oh my God, oh my God'*

Anne: *'Will you shut up please?'*

Me: *'Oh my God, oh my God, oh my God'.*

We had still yet to meet the owners and convince them that we would take good care of the place. They had never rented a place out, yet we were currently landlords to two places in London. One set of tenants were fine, whilst the other had almost completely ruined our flat that we had lovingly restored.

We had bought an Edwardian maisonette 8 years previously that was a beautiful shell on a stylish road just minutes from the centre of Muswell Hill, but inside it was a complete mess and probably hadn't been touched for a few decades. Over the course of three years we put back original fireplaces, redecorated throughout, restyled the balcony and small garden, put in a new kitchen and bathroom, walnut wooden floors throughout and much more. We thought it would be our forever home before my redundancy, but going back to see it once the new tenant was living there broke our hearts. It was ruined and the garden was like a jungle. I estimated the cost to redo the place to be well over £20,000.

Despite common opinion, being a landlord is not an easy business, not at all, unless you get lucky and find good tenants. Over the years we had generally been lucky - very lucky at times - but this wasn't one of those times. We thought it would be best not to mention that when we meet our prospective landlords, eh?

We also had to get our heads around the cost of moving. The rent that the owners wanted was double what we were currently paying and the electricity bill was likely to be far larger given the size of the place (200m²), although there was a working fireplace so hopefully there was no more need for those expensive halogen heaters. We both came to a fairly swift conclusion: let's do it for a year at least and see how we are at the end of it. If the worst comes to the worst at least we can say that we had lived in such an amazing place for a year; to hell with common sense.

We met the owners in late January and agreed terms. Now was just the tortuous wait until the end of April, when our current tenancy expired and we could move, although time passed fairly quickly getting all of our things together and boxed up.

The big question that was unanswered was how were we going to move our things up the mountain? Our part of Greece doesn't really have removal companies. There is also a law that I don't fully understand even now that means that you can't just hire a van and do it yourself as both of us have done before in the UK, nor are there 'man with a van' services. There was no way we could fit things in our car and even if we could it would probably mean 20-30 trips.

Then inspiration hit me: a big, strong friend owned an old white UK S-reg Ford Transit van, one that had seen a fair bit of use over the years. That is a polite way of saying it was highly illegal and probably shouldn't have been on the road. For example, the handle on the back doors had gone, so they were held together with rope looped through two holes in the door. I asked if I could pay him and a friend to help us move our stuff and he agreed.

Our new landlords kindly let us move in a few days early as they were heading back to the UK before our lease formally commenced. There comes a time in these parts of Greece, usually in March, where you know that for the next seven to eight months the weather will be lovely. Even days where it rains are enjoyed, giving gardens much needed moisture and resetting the temperatures several degrees lower. There also comes a point in time, usually around mid to late April, where almost at a flick of a switch that 'nice' weather turns into 'full-on baking summer' heat.

In 2012, that day was April 27th, the very day we were due to move - because it would, wouldn't it?

It took three trips up the mountain, praying that the van's back doors would remain closed, to move our stuff. On that one day we saw three very large snakes of about 4-6 ft long on our new road - what had we got ourselves into? I later found out that this was common. A Greek saying was that snakes came out of hibernation on 21st April, but in reality it can be weeks before that. As they are cold blooded animals they need the sun to warm them up. But the sun can only warm up one side, so it is common in the early days of summer for snakes to warm up one side with the sun and one side on the warm surface of the road.

There were then three further back breaking days where we put together furniture and arranged the house how we wanted it. At the end of each day we would relax on the terrace with a cold drink, still speechless at the view, soothing our aching feet in washing up bowls of soapy warm water like 'nans'.

With the inside of the house ready, we turned to the garden. It was too late to grow vegetables now until late September, but there was one major job that needed doing. The field next to us had grown from something that we could walk around in January when we first saw the house, to a jungle of 5 ft high grass. Our landlords had left a strimmer, so it was time to bite the bullet.

I started off and within maybe three minutes I had hit a rock and the strimming cord had broken. Take off visor, spend minutes working out how to replace the cord and start again. Then not even three minutes passed before it broke again. This process continued for five miserable hours. I have since learned that you should never let grass get this long - not our fault of course - and if it does get out of control to start cutting the grass from 1/3 of the way down and continue down, rather than trying to strim the bottom of the grass. It was an incredibly frustrating process, made harder by the heat, the irregular terrain and the visor.

There *may* have been a diva strop moments after the 25th breakage where the strimmer was launched into the next field. OK, in the interests of honesty, there *was* a diva strop. As I climbed over the dry stone wall to retrieve it I was reminded of my very short career of playing golf. I once watched a video of a man with similar 'skills' as myself try and hit the ball over the lake to the green. *Splash*. He put a new ball down, took a swing and *splash*. A third ball: *splash*. Infuriated, he threw his entire golf bag into the lake. You could then almost see his brain whirring, then he took his shoes off and waded into the lake. He dragged his golf bag out, unzipped the front pocket, got his car keys out … and then hoyed the bag once again back into the lake.

Such displays of annoyance are perfectly understandable in the heat of the moment, but ultimately futile. That said, I made myself a promise that I would never, ever strim a field again. And to this day I've stuck to that promise.

Welcome to the Jungle - the field, before…

…and after

One of the many joys of living here are the stray cats. There are several more 'formal' animal welfare groups, such as MIAO (Mani International Animal Organisation), together with several locals who feed the strays. As well as feeding the animals, rehoming those that can be found a loving forever home, they also operate a 'TNR' or 'Trap, Neuter & Return' operation. Animals are caught, neutered and then tagged before being released. The tag is a small section of the ear taken off, pain-free, to allow volunteers to identify which animals have already been neutered. Females can give birth to six or more kittens at a time, up to five times a year, so are the first ones to be searched for.

My good friend, our highly talented local vet Kostas, is instrumental in this and one day a year he provides his services for free for as many stray cats as can be caught. We are lucky to have him.

The tourist season, typically from May to October, brings rich pickings for the cats. Tourists feed them and tavernas are full for scrounging the odd piece of souvlaki or, if they are lucky, steak. But in the off season it is a tough life for the strays. Anne and I used to regularly head down to the sea front after work with a rucksack of food and would feed the many strays that were there. They were expert operators, they knew exactly who would yield to their charms and who wasn't worth the time. After a few months they got to know both Anne and I as 'soft touches'. We would feed them in out of the way places so as not to annoy certain taverna owners and then go on with our day. But often the cats would follow us, sometimes in large numbers.

Once, after having fed the cats, Anne and I decided to walk the bay from end to end. We were not alone however and as we passed a popular bar/café one of the customers shouted 'Bloody hell, it's the Pied Piper of Stoupa!' I turned around to see perhaps 25 of our stray cat crew following us. Given it was the winter and there were no tourists at all around it was quite the sight.

11th January 2015, my 41st birthday. Out of shot: another 20 cats. 'The Guy-ed Piper of Stoupa'?
Not very snappy, but I've been called far worse in my time.

The most confident and friendly strays will survive a number of years. They know how to play to us 'soft touches', sitting on laps, circling around ankles, just looking cute. But those of a more timid nature struggle and many sadly perish. I would estimate that a 'good' life of a stray cat here is just 4-6 years, perhaps less, so far less than half that of a pampered house cat. There are a number of factors - malnutrition, disease and cars are the main three.

In between organising the new house, working and throwing temper tantrums in the field, Anne and I spent a lot of time down in the bay. There was one tiny, malnourished kitten who we both loved. As soon as we turned the corner she would see us from 100 yards and run over, dance between our legs, tripping us up. We would feed her of course, but she wanted more than just food - she wanted affection, companionship, a lap to sit on. She was jet black, with emerald eyes.

The Greeks have a similar - silly - superstition to the UK that says black cats are unlucky. I think I am right in saying that black cats are the least likely to be rehomed from a UK shelter. Please, it is the 21st Century - haven't we gotten over that mumbo jumbo yet? One day, a few months after first seeing this kitten, it walked a few hundred metres over to a bar we were sitting outside and jumped on Anne's lap. We weren't even eating, all she wanted was companionship. While we were there Anne got an email - a new contract for her business, one she hadn't even pitched for! Now, please tell me just how unlucky black cats are?

The kitten jumped off Anne's lap and we paid and left. I knew what conversation we were shortly going to have, but I wanted Anne to start it rather than me. After all, it was me that 'sort of' asked if we could keep Jeeves, so it was time to even things up. (In later years people would sometimes accuse Anne of being the *'crazy cat lady'*. How sexist! It was almost always me! There does exist something called a *'crazy cat man'*!)

Sure enough, the conversation started. If we left this kitten, despite it being friendly towards humans, she might perish in the winter. Yes, but we have just got a new house and we had already shaved 20% off the number of cats we had when we told the landlords we only had four, when in fact we also had 'acquired' The Taliban, or perhaps more accurately, he acquired us. We can't get another! Ah, but our landlords are in the UK and will not be checking up on us and anyway, we are working flat out to repair the house and keep it and the grounds in wonderful shape, being model tenants. Yes, but they are friends with the neighbours - could we be reported and if so, is that a breach of contract, meaning that we would get turfed out of our lovely new dream house? But look at her! One more kitten, just one!

We decided to do a quick experiment, based a little on the game of Spoof, to decide what we should do. I could go into detail about strategy etc, but I'll be honest: it was designed so that I could get my way.

Rules: Two stones each taken from the beach, M&M size. We both turn away and each person can put anything up to the two stones in their right hand and then hold it up. Zero stones meant 'no, we cannot have this gorgeous friendly kitten'. One stone was 'maybe, I'm not averse to the idea of taking this gorgeous friendly kitten home and giving it an amazing life'. Two stones is 'Give. Me. The. Kitten.

Now'. (I did have a spare third stone hidden and ready to slip into my hand just in case things didn't go my way, naturally).

Three stones or more and we'd go for it. We both opened our palms on the count of three. Four stones - unanimous! The cat crew now numbered six. She had a lovely sparky personality so Anne, the 'crazy cat woman', decided she would call our new crew member Sparky.

Sparky, shortly after we brought her home

This was the time where we started to notice a pattern that would become familiar: the evolution from street cat to house cat. With every kitten that we took in since, we have followed the exact same routine:

1. Clean their ears for ear mites. Every street cat has them, they are very easily transferred to others. First, wash out their ears with a water spray, then let the cat shake its head. You will only make the mistake of doing this indoors once as they go everywhere. It clears 80% of the mites immediately, but there are others that are a little more resilient and for these you need to squeeze in a special cream that kills the mites.

2. Take the cat up to the bedroom with a litter tray and some food. Most kittens will not leave the bedroom for two to three weeks, just sleeping and eating. Staying alive on the street is a tiring, 24 hour a day job and they are almost always absolutely shattered.

3. Watch as they enter the 'Eddie Murphy in Trading Places' phase, where they can't quite believe this is happening to them, as in the scene where the Duke Brothers first show him his new house and he plays basketball with a priceless vase. Food on tap! Waiter service!

4. If they are old enough, they are then spayed, vaccinated and microchipped. We have two chip reading cat flaps in the house which keeps strays out and only lets our cats in.

5. Register the cat on the chip reader and wait for them to figure out how these things work.

6. Then they finally enter the world again, while we spend the week fretting whether they will be OK, forgetting that they have already spent months keeping themselves alive on the street in a much harsher environment before joining our crew.

7. Watch them enter their 'dragster' phase, where with a regular and plentiful supply of food they shoot up in size, but it always seems that the back legs grow much faster than the front, making them look like the iconic US racing cars. This has the effect that when running they almost seem to overtake themselves as the back is going faster than the front.

8. Repeat.

Chapter Ten: 2013, 'I rather like it here'

2013 was a year of just sitting back, starting to relax and enjoying our new surroundings. The end of this year, however, would dictate a lot of the following year.

Both Anne and I absolutely adored the new place. The increased rent wasn't hurting us too much financially and of course the cats absolutely loved it. We were right on the edge of hundreds of acres of Greek scrub land and olive groves, ripe for hunting. We started to receive regular 'presents', mostly dead, but also some alive. Rats, mice and shrews were common and occasionally we would get scorpions and snakes. I also witnessed Franklin trying to catch a foot long iguana.

Yes, we even had iguanas. Previously the only one I had seen was at my friend Rodger's house. Rodger was a lovely, calm mannered German and an IT genius. One day he completed a job for a client who told him 'I'm sorry, but I don't have any money, but here, you can take my pet iguana instead', so he did, and named her Josephine.

We decided to ask for an extension to our lease and were delighted when our landlords agreed. Now we would get to spend at least two years in our dream house.

One very hot day in July Anne and I went down to the bay for lunch at a favourite taverna. Most tavernas allow stray cats - we didn't tend to frequent the ones that didn't allow them that often. *H Avli tis Theanos* (known as '*The Yard*') had a whole band of strays and also served one of the best kleftika in the village. Later I will go into more detail about the best Greek food available and also give you my recipes so that you can recreate them, but for now all I will say is that it is a wonderful Greek dish with an interesting history … and I have a raging kleftiko habit.

Stoupa and Kalogria have roughly thirty tavernas, each doing their unique take on this dish. I had carried out a full and thorough kleftiko audit of each one of them - in the interests of science - and '*The Yard*' was in my top two.

We were greeted by the owner and sat down at the table ready to order. Almost immediately a tiny ginger male kitten jumped up on Anne's lap, staying there for the entire duration of the meal. He was so small, he could fit in the palm of your hand.

'No', I said, anticipating the coming question.

The owner came over with the bill and noticed the kitten on Anne's lap. 'Oh, he's gorgeous isn't he? He's got no family, I think he was just dumped down here. You wouldn't consider giving him a home?'

First it was cats that could spot our weakness, now you could add taverna owners to the list.

So we e took him home and started the now familiar routine for cat number seven. But what to call him? Male, ginger … Hucknall, let's call him Hucknall!

*The new boy, **Hucknall** (Huck, Ginge, Huckster, Huckerbee)*

I should set the record straight before you jump to any incorrect conclusions. Under no circumstances could I be described a fan of Simply Red. It was clear that Huck was going to be a big male and I've always wanted a big, fat, ginger cat called Hucknall. He's now approximately 6kg and still a lap cat. In fact he gets most annoyed if you have to stand up while he is on your lap, but lap action is strictly on his terms only. Huck is a big, lumbering oaf, with a 'tail of destruction' that knocks over anything that gets in the way - drinks, pens, money, bottles of wine, you name it. He's a fussy eater, a messy eater, a big clumsy clot and we absolutely adore him.

They say that once you get to 40 you know your own mind, but your body starts falling apart. I was a year short of the mark when an old injury reared its head. Many years before in my early 20s I went on a fairly disastrous snowboarding holiday in the French Alps. The week before we left I split up with my girlfriend who was also booked on the holiday but came along anyway, then on the first day I managed to tear the ligaments in my left foot doing a jump. It was a classic case of ambition not quite matching talent and upon landing my foot ripped the binding off the board. I spent the rest of the week on crutches drinking £5 cups of tea in overpriced cafes on the slopes while everyone else had a great time. Oh, and on the way back we were involved in a massive 30 car pileup on the motorway. We managed to brake before hitting a mass of crashed cars in front of us and could only watch and pray as others skidded their way towards us. Somehow the Gods were smiling on us: a couple of cars smashed into each other and formed a protective barrier around us, as others piled into them. We made it out shaken, but without a scratch.

I really should have had an operation, but my final year of university was upon me and I needed to be fairly mobile. Anyway, I was young, the body heals itself doesn't it? Sadly this youthful thesis turned out to be incorrect.

I woke up one morning in so much pain and thought my ankle had broken somehow. Anne drove me to a place where I had once served as unofficial receptionist for two years - Kalamata Hospital. I was x-rayed and out in 40 minutes, it was wonderful. No broken bones, but they suggested some physiotherapy.

I saw an advertisement for a physio on a local website and gave the lady a call. That afternoon I met Zefi for the first time. She's an ex-Olympian and a fantastic physiotherapist. She is also crazy in the best kind of way. She explained that there was a problem in my ankle, but that the problem also affected my foot and my knee. She also said that she had had similar problems before and that the treatment that she would have to give me was the most painful of any of her treatments. 'You will scream out loud' she said and, boy, she was not wrong.

I wanted to turn a negative into something at least vaguely positive, so I suggested that she teach me a new Greek swear word each session that I could scream out when the pain got too much. And that is how I became incredibly proficient at swearing in Greek. It's not really a topic you can ask your teacher to cover, is it? Thank you Zefi.

It is strange how ideas come to you, but one afternoon while I was watering the garden a song came on iPod shuffle by a band that I loved. They had been number one in the US and sold 19 million copies of their first album. To put that into perspective, at the time before Adele was even attending the BRITS school, the biggest selling album was Michael Jackson's 'Thriller' at 40 million. This band did half of that with their first record when they were not even 25!

Their second album was a stone cold classic, but the world just wasn't quite ready for it. I loved reading the stories of what they got up to. Imagine being number one in the US, touring the world, selling millions of records. The world is your oyster and they took advantage of every single minute of it. Their debauchery was legendary. This was a story that needed telling and I decided that I was going to be the one to tell it.

Have I mentioned before that Anne and I believe that that 'if you don't ask you don't get'? What is the worst that can happen if you ask politely?

Now I needed to work out how I was going to achieve this. My best mate worked in the music industry, he must know their manager? Through him I got his email address and asked him to pass on a message. A few days later one of the band members, let's call him 'DB', got in touch. We chatted for an hour on the phone about all sorts of things and he invited me over to the UK meet up. He lived in North Devon and my parents lived in Devon, so I figured I would combine the visit to both meet DB and see my parents, whilst also stopping off at my favourite curry house in Reading on the way. (If you ring them up and beg for them to stay open as your flight comes in late, mention that you are flying in from Greece specifically to eat their lovely food, it works!).

I spent an incredibly enjoyable afternoon at the house of one of my musical heroes in late October. We talked music, he told me some crazy stories, showed me all his platinum records and even a platinum cassette, which I never even knew existed. At the end of the evening I asked him if he would be happy for me to write his biography and he agreed, saying he would come over to Greece when time allowed. Result!

I left, absolutely buzzing and arrived back at my parents' house to hear the news that Lou Reed had died. In just one day I had met one musical hero and lost another.

Despite a few false starts the book still hasn't been written, but with all the stories I know to date, if and when it is finished it really will be *'Unbelievable'*.

Perhaps the high point of the year was a 2 day break we took to Elafonisos, a tiny island of just 19km^2 off the east coast of the 'third finger' of the Peloponnese, to the east of us.

Our interest in the area was piqued after watching a BBC documentary called Pavlopetri: The City Beneath the Waves. Pavlopetri was once a thriving trading outpost 3500 years ago before the sea submerged it, and it is said to be the inspiration for the story of Atlantis. It was rediscovered in the 1960s, but it has only recently been examined.

A team from Nottingham University painstakingly mapped the site using specialist cameras on surfboards. From that, you could see the ruins of houses, roads and storerooms. The BBC programme then used CGI, together with artefacts found on the site such as vases, to recreate what the city would have looked like in its heyday. Piecing together the clues they concluded that it was a major trading hub, exchanging goods from places such as Crete and North Africa.

Best of all, it was only a few metres underwater, so even if you couldn't scuba dive, a simple snorkel and mask would do. To have something like this just on your doorstep was too much temptation and it was an utterly fabulous experience.

The entire documentary is available to watch on YouTube and is thoroughly recommended. It can be found by simply searching for its title as mentioned above.

We went back to Sunderland for Christmas to see Anne's parents and sister. It is never easy leaving our mountain and was made even harder by the fact that we now owned seven cats. Luckily a lovely couple had moved in behind us and they adored cats. In fact, pretty much everyone around us had cats. They offered to look after our crew while we were away.

Anne's parents were both in their late 80s and unable to travel and as Kalamata airport is only open in the tourist season so the journey at Christmas is a particularly long one: the drive to Athens Airport from Stoupa (now 4 hours, reduced from 5.5 due to the aforementioned new motorway, at last completed), wait there for two hours, fly to Schiphol Airport (3.5 hours), wait an hour or two for the connection to Manchester (1.5 hours) then drive to Sunderland (3.5 hours). In total it was about 15 hours of travel, but it was worth it. I cooked us all Christmas dinner and we all got rather merry.

As they were now living in sheltered housing, we stayed at a B&B on the coast at Roker, a couple of miles outside Sunderland City Centre, which did the most amazing fry-ups. It was a lovely way to end the year, yet unknown to us, it would define the first four months of next year.

Chapter Eleven: 2014, Howard's Way

One of the many advantages of living on a deserted mountainside in Greece is that we never, ever get ill. We don't have to commute in packed Tube carriages, we don't have kids coming back from school with all sorts of illnesses and we rarely interact socially with anyone else.

There is one exception to this rule however, and that is when we have to spend hours in a big metal tube 30,000ft up in the air. Perhaps because we don't get ill our immune systems are weaker, I don't know, but every time, without fail, we would get a cold after having been on a plane.

Anne started feeling ill when we were in Sunderland. I started feeling the same by the time we got through security at Manchester Airport. We both felt absolutely terrible by the time we landed in Athens. When I say 'terrible' I mean 'so bad that we considered getting a hotel as we weren't sure if we could make it home' terrible.

We finally made a decision to go for it and took turns at driving. Luckily while one of us was feeling awful the other was OK and we switched seats a couple of occasions during the trip back in the dark and the rain. By the time we reached Kalamata I was in an absolutely terrible state, shivering despite the heating being on full and covered by a jumper and a coat. This was bad, it was really bad.

The drive from Kalamata back to our house is a tough one, even in daylight. But in the dark, with heavy rain and what we now suspected to be 'flu, it was horrible. Thankfully Anne drove this part of the journey as I was now hallucinating, alternating between extreme heat and extreme cold and apparently singing the theme tune to 80s TV yachting show 'Howard's Way' - at least that is what Anne later told me, I have no recollection.

It was a good decision to make a dash for it from Athens, as once we got home we just dumped our suitcases in the living room and stayed in bed for almost two whole weeks. The Sofitel room rates at Athens

Airport are about €150 a night and room service is upwards of €20 a meal - not that we were eating - so that would have been quite a hefty bill.

Anne recovered OK, but for the next four months I would be sleeping 14-18 hours a day as my body tried to rid itself of this wretched virus, post viral fatigue syndrome. It was debilitating.

When I finally managed to make it out of bed I had done some thinking and decided to chance my arm with our landlord - would he let us keep some chickens? He kindly said that he had always wanted to keep chickens and the field was perfect for it, so go right on ahead.

My new neighbours liked the idea too and offered to go 50/50 on both the costs and the duties. I spoke with a friend and he agreed to get us six hens and also to build a coop. When the coop arrived it was obvious that he had used whatever paint he had lying around for the outside and there it was, part pink, part yellow. It looked like Mr Blobby. We were all aghast, it wasn't *quite* what we had been expecting. We soon had it varnished in dark brown to blend in with the nearby oak tree.

We built them a run and started enjoying eggs with bright orange yolks. Once you've had your own eggs you really cannot buy eggs from the supermarket ever again.

We then had to name them and as I suspect you have gathered by now, we were experts at coming up with stupid names for animals, so they were named The Colonel, Nando, Dixie etc.

That week we let them out into the field to chase crickets, dust bath and peck away at the ground as chickens do. When it was time for them to be put away we discovered that new hens aren't the easiest to catch. It took four of us, one with a net that was used for rock pooling and the others waving around an olive net, about 90 minutes to catch them all. If only we had videoed it, we could have sped it up into a two minute film and put the Benny Hill theme tune over it.

The next week we let them out again. At around midday we heard a terrible sound - a fox had got into the field and killed five of our girls. Only The Colonel survived. It was a bitter and costly lesson.

Looking back with what I know now, we were stupidly naïve. We live next to over a thousand acres of wild mountain terrain, *of course* there would be foxes. I kick myself to this day. They were under my watch and I had failed them.

In the next chapter I will give a brief guide to properly keeping chickens with all that I have learned, I hope you find it helpful and I hope it stops you making the stupid mistakes I did.

I was still trying to shake this virus and in the background the Greek political and economic situation was still dire. There was talk of a possible Greece leaving the EU - *Grexit* - and personally I thought it was highly likely. It was the 'best' option out of several terrible options. When presented with a tray of turd sandwiches and forced to choose one, you go for the one with the thickest bread. Against this backdrop we decided that there was only one logical move: we should buy a house!

To be fair, it was actually not as stupid an idea as it sounded. The finances worked, it was our dream house and I've always believed that if you want to do something and you can, then why wait? There are too many times I can remember that the stars have aligned, yet I have procrastinated, only for the opportunity to be gone when I finally got my arse in gear to do it. Not this time.

We knew our landlords wanted to sell and we had a longstanding offer to buy our flat in London. More importantly, we couldn't ever envisage living in the UK again - we wanted to spend the rest of our years in this house on this mountainside.

We made some calls and within 30 minutes we had agreed to sell our flat in London and buy this house! I told you Anne and I don't mess around!

It's probably best to gloss over the sale and purchase themselves as neither of them were straightforward, even by 'normal' standards. This wasn't because of the Greek system for buying and selling property, these were more 'man-made' problems.

It took about four months to exchange and completion finally took place on a blisteringly hot August day in Kalamata. Our lawyer was magnificent and took us through the whole process with expert precision. One of the peculiarities of Greek property law is that a fair amount of the deal is done in cash - even the Notary is paid in cash. This explains how I was walking around Kalamata with a little over €21,000 in cash in my rucksack.

Loadsamoney: Waiting to pay the Notary and buy the house, Kalamata, August 2014.

Whereas both Anne and I have previously nervously waited for funds to clear in the UK in a removals van in the rain outside properties, this time we just swam in the sea waiting for funds to clear. We finally got the news - we now owned a piece of Greece!

The view from the ground floor terrace

An already surprising year had yet one more surprise up its sleeve. We went out to a favourite taverna for their closing day. The owners were going to take a month or so off after that day to recuperate after the summer season and then spend the next few months olive harvesting. This was a fairly standard routine for many of the taverna owners. Pressed olive oil would first be used for the taverna and the rest sold to the local co-operative at varying prices, roughly €3.5-€4 a litre. Compare that to what Waitrose charge for finest Kalamata olive oil!

I had my usual lamb souvlaki, a huge kebab of meat that curled around a plate full of piping hot chips and salad. We ate and drank and then were suddenly aware of a tiny, malnourished kitten at our feet. We fed it scraps of food as was customary. The taverna owner told us that he loved the little thing, had taken pity on it and fed it every day, but he was worried about her as this was the last day the taverna was open for the season and he wouldn't be about to feed her any more. Well, I think you can see where this is going?

Meet Boomer, cat number eight.

Boomer (Booms, The Boomese Triangle ... running out of inspiration now)

Booms is an incredibly independent cat, semi-feral. She will go out for three to four days usually, then come back demanding food and cream - Boomer loves cream. Then she will sit on Anne's lap for an evening, maybe spend the night up away on the cat walkway we built on our living room wall, or sometimes just go out straight away after food. One August she went missing for over a week. We were incredibly worried as August heat is brutal, often well over 40 degrees and there is no water about. The week turned to ten days, twelve days, fourteen days and we feared the worst. We emailed around friends and neighbours, posted on local Facebook sites to see if anyone had seen her, but nothing. Something bad must have happened to her.

Then after sixteen days she wandered in as if nothing had happened, demanding food and cream. We later found out that one of the areas that she would hang out in had a holiday home with an automatic watering system, timed to go off twice a day. That was where she was getting her water!

Chapter Twelve: A Short Guide to Keeping Chickens

Keeping chickens is a noble pastime, one that gives me a lot of pleasure and also has nice rewards. I've kept them for six years now and can't foresee a time when I will stop.

Getting started isn't too hard or expensive. While we now have built a large walk in coop, we started out with the Mr Blobby construction my friend made, but coops can easily be bought flat packed and assembled in an hour or so, so we when acquired more hens we bought a coop online from Germany that came to a little over €200 including postage. It is a good idea to set the coop up a foot or so off the ground to stop any water getting in and also to give the hens a place to hide from the sun. If you place the coop next to a fence, be aware that the hens will fly up onto the roof of the coop and can then escape over the top. We put an olive net over ours.

You will need to have a well-protected run for them, as big as you can spare. It is often a good idea to check how rainfall flows through your field. I wish we knew that when we chose our location as we managed to choose the worst position going, a place where much of the mountain's rainwater runs off, meaning the hens have a water feature in winter and putting them away is a treacherous activity.

We bought steel poles and set them in concrete, then put approximately 8 ft of chicken wire around the structure, digging down a little over a foot and setting the chicken wire into the ground with stones from the field and concrete on top, stopping it from being dug up. Foxes and other animals are incredibly inventive in their methods to try and gain access, so you need to check the perimeter of the run regularly to make sure no access is being gained through one form or another.

In the height of the Greek summer it is essential that they always have sufficient water and shade - I have two water butts, so if one runs out the other is there. A bowl of water won't do as it will be quickly knocked over. We have shade under the coops, plus there is a large olive tree that I keep unpruned to give more shade.

There are a number of predators you need to look out for, foxes being the main one, but there are also jackals and pine martens. Foxes are as wily as their reputation suggests and once they get into a coop they won't just take what they need, they will kill everything in sight. I absolutely adore foxes and will never understand how people can hunt them down and tear them apart as 'sport'. It disgusts me. However, my obligations lie with my hens and so I do everything that is humane to keep the foxes away.

One thing I have been told is that foxes are not like cats when it comes to climbing, so if there are trees near the coop it is unlikely that they will be used to scale the fence.

Unfortunately you need to be mentally prepared that it is likely a fox attack will happen and when it does it is devastating. You also need to accept that you might have to put an animal out of its misery, as I had to after a jackal attacked one of my girls. It still haunts me to this day, but I know it was the right thing to do for the time.

Don't worry about snakes with the hens. Hens can be vicious at times, not to humans, but I have seen several snakes meet their maker around my girls.

I have always gone for just hens, no cockerels. I'd love a big, majestic cockerel, but I'm not sure my other neighbours would be amused. They really are incredibly loud at many times of the day. You don't need them for egg production, they are more ornamental in my view. I still want one though.

Each hen costs around €7. When you consider a free range egg is 50c in the supermarket and a hen lives for three years, maybe more, even accounting for your fixed costs and feed, they make more financial sense than my cats! I've been racking my brains for ways to monetise the cats for the last ten years to no avail - we spend more on cat food in a month than we do on the mortgage for our flat in London.

Chicken food is generally milled corn, a sack of which costs €15 and is so big it is hard to carry. I then supplement that with vegetable offcuts from meals and a tin of sweetcorn in the morning. As and when salad or other vegetables I am growing go to seed I also give them those, plus any windfall figs or prickly pears.

In summer I also get a tray that I cook my Yorkshire puddings in and pour out a tin of sweetcorn into the mould, topping each one up with water and put them in the freezer. In the harsh summer they absolutely adore these frozen treats. I call them '*chook ices*'.

A standard summer breakfast for my girls: Garden offcuts and a bowl of 'Chook Ices'

Once the hens are of laying age, six months approximately, you should get one egg a day per hen. This slows down at certain points of the year, August and also around December. It also slows down when the hen gets older, but by then they have earned a nice Mediterranean retirement.

At one stage I was getting 15 eggs a day quite regularly, over 100 a week. Eggs are a fantastic currency here and I used to swap the excess eggs with my local veggie van that came around, meaning I could get any vegetables and fruit I wasn't growing, for 'free'.

Our little hamlet not only has a lot of cat lovers, it also has people with fruit trees and vegetable plots. We operate an informal scheme where if anyone has gluts - inevitable - they hand them out, so I will often leave a dozen or so eggs on my neighbours' gates and in return get bags of oranges, lemons or vegetable offcuts. It works like a treat and it is lovely to open your gate and find a surprise waiting for you.

Sometimes, typically in young hens, you can get double yolker eggs. An average supermarket egg weighs about 65g, but ours are more like 70g-80g. Once we got a triple yolker weighing 105g! I understand the odds of that are something akin to winning the lottery. We fried it up and had it on toast - two pieces of toast.

Triple yolker!

Oh and the taste! Did I mention the taste? You can never buy shop bought eggs ever again once you keep your own hens. The yolks are deep orange and just taste amazing. I tend to favour them boiled with soldiers, a twist of salt on the top. I've even refined this further and now buy bacon flavoured TUC biscuits for easier dipping - bacon and egg!

Maintenance is fairly quick. You need to let them out into the pen by about 8am and lock them back up safely in their coop around sunset. They will put themselves away at sunset after a while. This is one downside of keeping hens - you are fairly restricted regarding timings, but it's not a problem to put them away earlier if you have plans. If you go on holiday for example it is extremely helpful to have friendly neighbours - we go 50/50 with our immediate neighbour on the mountain and can always swap weeks or certain days if we have other plans.

They need cleaning once a day and for small things they sure can create a lot of mess! This is invaluable however, don't dispose of it. Chicken poo is perhaps the best manure you can get, but it cannot be put directly onto vegetables as it will kill them - it must be broken down, ideally in a compost heap over 6-9 months.

There is a rather pleasing circularity to it all. I harvest my vegetables, salad and fruit, cook us meals and give the chickens the offcuts. They, in turn, give us eggs and create amazing compost to put on the next season of fruit and vegetables. Each tree in the orchard, whether olive or citrus fruit, gets a large dump of compost at its base twice a year, courtesy of my girls.

Their breakfast is vegetable offcuts, windfall figs, prickly pears, chook ices and a tin of sweetcorn. I buy the very best feed for them which gives a greater egg yield. After several years of using the Mr Blobby coop and the flat pack German coop, together with a friend we built a 3m x 2m walk-in coop with five nesting boxes. It's lovely and cool all day and even has its own artwork (more on that later).

They have several dedicated dust bath areas and more shade from a large olive tree. This tree was planted at the same time as all of the others, but is now 50% bigger than any of the others, a testament to the powers of chicken poo compost. The tree was originally outside the first run, but I decided to make the run far larger and now it sits inside. The front of the run is just chicken wire so they can look at the Mediterranean and there is a lovely tall stone wall at the back.

I run a watering system for all the trees which saves a lot of time. It is on a timer, twice a day and means that the water soaks into the ground exactly where I want it, rather than the scattergun approach of a hose. I've run a line off this and there is now a water outlet hanging from the olive tree, so twice a day the hens get a chicken shower.

Lastly, I normally plant 30-40 lettuces and invariably some go to seed or aren't great. Using a souvlaki stick we skewer a hole in the base of the lettuce and tie it up on the olive tree with string so it is hanging down about a foot off the ground - a *lettuce piñata.*

The hens are let out once a day while I clean them out and also whenever we are working in the field. In summer there are crickets to catch, new plants to peck at and dust baths.

Whilst in the summer it is too hot, in spring and autumn it is absolutely lovely to sit out after a day of work with a cold drink, the chickens all around us, and the cats as well. The cats are no bother whatsoever - if they get too close they get a peck for their troubles and put firmly in their place.

Spring brings huge amounts of new growth in the field as well as gorgeous wild flowers. Much of this can be given to the chickens - wild horta (green leaves) and numerous other plants/weeds. An easy rule is to let them out around this time and just watch what they go for. Certain plants they just won't touch, but others they adore - free food!

Some guests have said that I spoil my hens. Is there any truth in this? Hell yes!

Chapter Thirteen: 2015, Grand Designs

Both Anne and I love watching Grand Designs and now it felt like we were in our own episode. Someone posted their version of the Grand Designs bingo card online, where you could check off each cliché, one by one: run out of funds, project running way beyond timetable, wrong sized windows, 'we'll be in by Christmas', arguments etc. By the end of this year we had pretty much checked off each one, with the welcome exception of 'unplanned pregnancy'.

We put in for planning permission for the installation of a swimming pool the previous year and were given a rough estimate of 'several months'. But then we hit a snag. I won't bore you too much with the complexities and absurdities of Greek planning law, but there is a rule often referred to as the 800m rule which was our first challenge. Greece doesn't want villages to spread out too far and so it has a rule that if you live within an 800m radius of the church spire pretty much anything goes. If you live outside of this you can only build a house of approximately 200m^2 on a plot of 4,000m^2 or larger - a huge plot.

We knew from when we bought the house the previous year that we were *right* on the boundary; so much so that if our house was built 10cm further south it would have had to have been demolished (the authorities are incredibly strict on this and similarly with building on 'Forestry' land). The pool area was just outside of the village zone. In addition, there was a gorge several hundred metres in front of us and the planning authorities said that no building could occur near the gorge. The fact that houses and pools were already there didn't seem to matter.

I turned down a friend's kind offer to 'move' the church spire on the topographical map as I wanted to do this properly. We were asked to do a second topographical plan, at a cost of €300, then a third. This went on for about eleven months. I was running out of patience and finally asked my architect 'do they just want an envelope with cash in it? Is that what they want?' She said that it was just the way, they weren't looking for *fakilaki* - literally brown paper envelopes and basically bribes - this was just the way it was.

They decided that they needed to do a site visit and drove two hours for a visit that lasted less than three minutes. They then granted us permission immediately.

Meanwhile Anne and I started work on the interior of the house, redecorating everything, putting a roll-top bath out on the terrace and taking down one of the *three* kitchens we had inherited.

The bath was wonderful. There is complete privacy and soon we had our first baths outside watching swallows flying around with the mountains and sea in the background.

A bath with a view

How anyone could think they need three kitchens I don't know, but that is one of the lessons learned out here - keep an eye on your builder at all times. A local volunteer firefighting group, who provide other charitable services, GAIA, took everything - including the kitchen sink - and reinstalled it the house of an elderly Greek man down the coast who was in need of a kitchen.

We also decided to put the field to good use and planted about 25 trees, with some help. Later in the book I will devote a small section to what I have learned about growing fruit and vegetables, plus all of the mistakes that I made. I was glad to have had some local help on this project as there is a special way to plant trees that I didn't know about and if I had ploughed on ahead everything might have died.

We already had a few fig trees, a pear tree, three very mature olive trees and some wild almond trees. Added to that we put in another eight olive trees for oil, two olive trees for eating olives, six orange/tangerine trees, a lemon, pomegranate and two grapefruit trees, one a blood grapefruit. I later added in three peach trees, a lime tree and a Jacaranda, sometimes known as a 'Prince' tree due to its lovely purple flowers that show up twice a year. No fruit from this one, just beauty. To add some definition to the field I also planted four Cypress trees.

In mid-June the Greek debt crisis reared its ugly head again once again. A certain UK newspaper that I detest had a headline reading 'Greece Burns!' People were getting in touch asking if we were OK, whether they should still come out on holiday, whether there were the reported food shortages, if there was civil unrest? The reality was that there were demonstrations - some violent - in Athens and

Thessaloniki, but really nowhere else. Athens is four or five hours by car away, Thessaloniki is nine.

I took photos and posted them on Facebook of the packed shelves in the supermarket, empty queues at the ATM etc. It was often infuriating how the whole economic crisis was being reported, even at times in the 'more trustworthy' UK news channels. The Guardian reported petrol shortages and loads of petrol stations closed in Kalamata, on the very day I drove all the way through there. There was not a single station shut, it was just an outright lie.

Closer to home, work started on the pool before we even had the final quote in, which didn't bode well. We had decided on a 10m x 5m infinity pool with heaters so we could use the pool all year round. The cover was sufficiently stable to take the weight of a cat, which was our number one priority.

Our architect had agreed with the owner of the land next door for access to our garden through for the heavy digging equipment as on this mountain you are digging almost solely into solid rock. On the day the diggers arrived, the owner also showed up with a demand: €5,000 in cash before the work could start.

The architect and builder both immediately said no, in perhaps more colourful language than that. Quite rightly, they had to think of future projects and didn't want to set a local precedent. They proposed that they would dig it out with pneumatic drills, at further cost to us, albeit not their fault in the slightest. If I had building experience I would have known that this was akin to emptying a bath with a teaspoon, but naïve as I was, I agreed. It took weeks - actually, scratch that - months longer than planned.

It was time for our first guests as homeowners to arrive, an old colleague/boss and his wife. He and I had worked together between 1998 and 2005 at a place that was a stupid amount of fun. You'll notice that I am not using names here and there is a very good reason for that.

I went for a job interview in the City of London in early 1998 and was actually interviewed by someone who I now count as a good friend. After the second interview the three candidates were taken to the pub to meet other people at the company. I was determined not to be the one that left first and stayed to the end with one other chap. Apparently the bar bill for that night stretched to over one metre long.

I said goodbye, desperately hoping that I had secured the job and got on a train from Paddington back to Reading, where I was living with my parents having finished university. I woke up in Bristol. A £90 taxi home sorted that one out which was a big hit to the finances. Worse than that, it was the *second* time that week I had done that, after meeting my London based old housemate for 'just a few' over the weekend.

When my mobile rang the next morning it was another one of those moments that you look back on and realise it completely changed the course of your life. I had been given the job! I desperately tried to sound enthusiastic, but in reality I had a monster hangover and couldn't wait to get back to bed.

Despite the interview I still had a feeling that life was going to end, get serious, and that my fun days of University were over. It was time to become an adult.

I couldn't have been more wrong. The place was rammed full of the biggest reprobates I have had the pleasure of knowing in my life. At 11am on my first day the boss of the desk said 'Come on, smoke break'. We walked outside the building and rather than hover outside like the rest, headed left along Old Broad Street and down the stairs to a much missed hostelry, Bill Bentleys, the scene of my interview, where the barmaid was already decanting a bottle of red wine for us. We had that in 30 minutes with a few cigarettes and chatted.

An hour after I got back to my desk I was dragged out again - kicking and screaming - to be taken for a curry by the 15 or so people on my desk to welcome me; three more pints.

I was lucky to work in that environment and through those years of the late 1990s. We had a dress down policy in effect years before it became the norm - no suits and not just on Fridays. I have no idea how my team got away with what we did. I guess it was because, despite appearances, they were the best team in the country at what they did and I was along for the ride, learning fast.

Perhaps it was also because we had a boss that really had no authority. He also lacked basic IT skills, once calling up the IT department and saying that the battery on his mouse mat had died, when in fact the mouse lead had just disconnected. He used to type out a letter, print it, not save the document and then ask his secretary to type it up!

Most lunch times would be at the pub playing pool and table football and most evenings carried on at a bar across the road. I still averaged about 60-70 hours a week at work however, as I was on the bottom rung and that was 'the done thing'.

One lunch time, things carried on so long that we got back to our desks at about 5pm. The aforementioned secretary had joined us at the pub and was in such a state that she opened up the coat cupboard and got in it, thinking it was the lift.

The lovely, fun private company that I joined inevitably got sold, to a FTSE 100 firm of outsourcing parasites and things changed. It was still a lot of fun, but in ever decreasing amounts. I hung on in there for another few years, but was rapidly losing faith in it. I loved my colleagues, loved my work, but disliked my employer for a myriad of reasons.

I took another job elsewhere and wrote out my resignation letter. Before I could hand it in I noticed on my Reuters screen that there was talk of 'power surges' at Aldgate Tube station, but I suspected something more was afoot and was sadly proved right: it was July 7th 2005. This was perhaps not the best day to resign, but I had to as by then, my girlfriend and colleague Anne - later to become my wife - and I had booked to go on holiday the next day. What a horrible day to be in London, the atmosphere was one of fear and we were all so relieved that we, as well as our family, friends and colleagues were lucky enough to have stayed safe.

Despite this, I went ahead and resigned - they were fuming - and the next day Anne and I left for our first trip to Kefalonia, unknowingly starting our love affair with Greece.

When I started my new job my former employers were fuming even more as fairly quickly I cost them lucrative business by winning a number of contracts that they were also bidding for. What was I to do? It was my job to do this kind of work, but I must admit it was quite satisfying.

I mentioned at the start of this book that before we made the decision to move to Greece I had been waiting on the final offer for another job. I waited three months having all but been promised the job and then just got a very short 'sorry, no can do' email. This led Anne to say 'sod it, shall we move to Greece?'

Fast forward to 2015 and over many a late night wine my house guest and former colleague told me what had happened in the background back in 2010, things I had never known. Apparently my old boss, still smarting, had heard I was going to be offered this job, with an organisation that he had a commercial relationship with, and he told them that if they employed me then their lucrative deal would be terminated.

Unwittingly he had just given us that final push that we needed to decide to move to Greece. He'll probably never know just how grateful the two of us are for his spiteful and unprofessional actions!

Once our visitors had left it was back to the house renovations. We had received a fair quote of around €1,000 for a polytunnel to be built in the garden, 4m x 6m. It took approximately three weeks to complete and now meant that we could now grow vegetables all year around. The sides would be lifted in the June - September period to keep the heat down.

In the next chapter I will give you some tips that I have learned through trial and error and ones taught to me by locals regarding growing fruit and vegetables and preserving what you have grown.

The first sparse crops grown in the tunnel - tomatoes, peppers, courgettes and salad.

Towards the end of the year we did our usual trip down the mountain to nearby Pantazi Beach to collect wood. We usually wait for a storm to wash driftwood up and then go down the next day. In just 45 minutes we could fill the entire boot with kindling.

There was of course one other advantage of heading down to this particular beach. An English couple who live near Pantazi, Chris and Sue, have been running a cat shelter down there for many years in tough conditions and at the time had something like 45 cats, of varying ages. They do their very best to get cats neutered and despite some kind donations do most of it out of their own pocket. They are a fantastic couple.

We filled the car up with free firewood and popped over the road to see our friends and check out the cats. One of the many issues that they have with running the shelter is that some people don't like it being there. A further issue is that once people know that it is there they just dump unwanted cats there, further increasing the burden on Chris and Sue.

We said hello and saw that they were bottle feeding a very small ginger and white kitten. He had been dumped with his brother, called Mouse. This little chap was so friendly and purry, we instantly fell for him. He had been named Squiggle because he was born with a deformed tail that looked like a cross between a rabbit and a pig's tail. When he ran he looked like a bunny rabbit. Oh, he was just gorgeous, but we already had seven cats, way too many.

Over the next few days we couldn't stop thinking of this gorgeous, tiny cat. He was being put in a box at night with his brother because he was so tiny they were worried that he could be attacked by foxes, jackals, pine martens or other larger cats.

Poor 'Squiggle' on the day he was dumped at Pantazi Beach Cat Shelter.

Indeed it was thought likely that he would never grow to full size due to his deformities. It seemed as if both of us were having the same thoughts and so we dropped Chris and Sue a line and asked if we could give Squiggle a new home.

We picked him up and brought him back to ours, starting - once again - the transformation from street cat to house cat. He slept on my pillow every night for weeks. We both liked the name Squiggle, but felt that a more regal name was appropriate and so we eventually renamed him Chester (*Bunny Bum, Chesterfield, Pumpkin, Pumpers, Pumping Station*). Cat number NINE!

Chester's first meal as a house cat - Warm line caught Alaskan pollock.

For a while first though, we referred to him as 'Aunty Cathy'. My Aunt Cathy had come over to house sit for a while when we went back to the UK to see Anne's parents. Cathy is a fantastic lady, so much fun, with endless energy. A holiday for her isn't your average package holiday. She'll go trekking in Peru or canoeing in Himalayan rapids.

When we returned from the UK she said she'd had a great time, but 'please, don't get any more cats because I and everyone else here think you are crazy'. Her, of all people, calling *me* crazy!? It reminded me of the story once of Keith Richards walking backstage and bumping into Shane McGowan of The Pogues who was somewhat worse for wear. Keith apparently told Shane to 'calm it down a bit'. If 'Keef' told you that, you'd have to take a long, hard look at yourself and your life choices!

Anyway, we both decided that if we got another cat we would name it after her, and so for a while before he was renamed Chester he was called 'Aunty Cathy'.

Oh, he was gorgeous! In fact he still is, although he's incredibly impatient. Anne and I rarely sleep in beyond 6am anyway, but on the odd occasion we have had a late night he wakes us up, demanding food or treats in a not too subtle way. Anne keeps a number of things on her bedside table and to get our attention he knocks each one off with his paw.

BANG! *Air conditioning control hits the floor, batteries fly everywhere*

BANG! *Hand cream hits the floor, to be used as a football if we ignore him*

BANG! *There goes the TV remote*

BANG! *Tissue box hits the floor* (Not as loud as the previous items, but he's running out of things to knock over now).

I find it hard to believe that some people claim that the Earth is flat - I mean, didn't they see the photos taken from the Moon? (Oh, sorry, no, those were faked weren't they?!) I would make a bet that any 'Flat Earther' doesn't own a cat. Why? Because if the world were flat it would have nothing on it as cats would have knocked everything off!

Anne and I adore all of our cats, but it's not against the law to sometimes get annoyed with them and this is one of those cases. Can we JUST FOR ONCE have a 30 minute lie in? Apparently not. I know what you are going to say - 'lock the door, stupid'! Yeah, we tried that, they just scratch at it instead. I know, insist Anne has what my old work insisted on - and I never complied with - a 'clear desk policy'. Ewww, I hate that phrase. Anyway, I have suggested it and on the rare few times that Anne has listened, Chester uses technique number two: whiskers thrust up the nostril. You just can't win. Neither can you hold it against him for more than a minute because he is Just. Too. Cute.

We have a phrase that we use when the cats are playing up, like this. M-CAD: 'My Cat's A Dick'.

Chapter Fourteen: Hints on Growing Fruit and Vegetables, Preserving your Crops & Foraging for Food

There is nothing better than eating food you have grown or foraged yourself - fresh, tasty and cheap. Back in London I used what available outdoor space we had to grow tomatoes, herbs, strawberries, potatoes, beans, mange tout etc. But growing vegetables in Greece is very different to the UK. Here is a list of tips to get you started, learned mainly by trial and error:

1. Throw Out Your Rule Book!

The theory remains the same - good soil, regular watering, sunlight, protection from pests - but the implementation is very different. In the UK I would wait until there was only a small chance of a frost and plant. In our area of Greece there has only ever been one frost in ten years. The abundance of sunlight and different seasons mean that planting times are earlier and the time available to grow is far greater; in fact with a polytunnel you can pretty much grow all year round, with the exception of August and two weeks either side of it.

Allow 6-8 weeks to propagate seeds, or buy ready propagated in your first year to make things easy. If there are propagated versions of crops for sale in the garden centre it means they are ready to plant, so I use this as a guide. I plant the following crops using this rough timetable:

January	Tomatoes (propagated from seed), salad, lettuces (in polytunnel)
February	Tomatoes (propagated from seed), salad, lettuces (in polytunnel)
March	Tomatoes, mange tout, peas (in polytunnel), onions, peppers, coriander (propagated from seed)
April	Courgettes

May	Nothing
June	Nothing
July	Melons
August	NOTHING - way too hot!
September	Broccoli, cauliflower
October	Potatoes (first crop, 90 days)
November	Nothing
December	Potatoes (second crop, 90 days)

2. Invest in a Polytunnel

This is not essential - I don't know of any Greeks that have one and they manage just fine - but I find it extends the growing window by a few months and gives you a good place to propagate crops. I have a set-up of several old shelving units to allow up to 20 trays of propagating seeds. The other advantage is that it gives protection from extreme wind and hail storms. You can be guaranteed to get one of the other - or both - once a year and I've lost numerous crops to them.

Our polytunnel took three weeks to build, at a cost of €1,000.

3. Pests

Whilst most English gardeners don't have to cope with 100km/h winds, there are other pests that make life incredibly difficult - slugs, snails etc. The good news is that they don't exist here to any significant degree. I might have seen one snail in ten years. It really makes life easier.

In Greece the only 'pest' I have witnessed is much cuter and far more welcome - tortoises! - although several friends have had packs of wild boar ruin crops.

Whilst perhaps not really classed as a pest, the extremely high winds and hail we get every year also need to be considered.

4. Copy the Greeks!

Pretty much every Greek with some outside space has a vegetable garden and they have centuries of knowledge passed down through generations - copy them! There are several amazing vegetable patches in the village and I often go down to see what they are doing and at what time of the year, and to pick up handy tips to use in my own garden. As soon as they start planting a crop I do the same. I look at how the crops are planted, what structures they climb up and where they are positioned relative to the sun. In July for example I noticed that many Greeks build a simple structure around most crops and drape over an olive net to give shade from the scorching heat.

I noticed that courgettes obviously need some shade from the heat and these are often planted underneath olive trees, at the base. I also saw that when broccoli is ready to harvest the Greeks only cut the main flower off, leaving the stem in the ground. The broccoli then grows in smaller florets from other parts of the plant. An old man in the village told me he gets an extra 25% or more broccoli from doing this.

5. Try Different Things

I try and keep the crops that I grow different from those I can buy in the supermarket if possible, so this year I grew purple mange tout, black peppers, different varieties of salads and loofahs for the bath.

Try and make the growing a mixture of inside and outside, experiment with two sets of the same crop to see which one works the best. If there is a pepper you like in the supermarket take the seeds from it, dry them and label them and try planting them. Our best melons are grown using dried seeds from supermarket bought melons.

6. Stagger Crops

Staggering planting means that you avoid gluts. I tend to plant ten lettuces, then two to three weeks later another ten, then a further ten a few weeks after that. If you do get a glut, which is almost inevitable, I give them to my neighbour who also grows and I get some of their glut later on in the year. The other alternative to giving it away is preserving.

7. Preserving Crops

I'm no expert here unfortunately, but the internet has helped immensely. Whenever we have a glut I Google 'ways of preserving X' and it's been fairly good so far. At one time I was picking a huge washing up bowl of tomatoes a day, so one day I made ketchup, the next few weeks I made load after load of passata. Sun dried tomatoes are easy too - slice in half, take out the pips and place in a glass dish. Cover with kitchen roll and … the Greek way is to leave them in your car! You do have the smell of tomato in there for a few days, but there are worse smells. Store in a jar away from the sun, with olive oil covering them.

Eggs are easily frozen too - just whisk them and add salt and pepper and put in a freezer bag, they will last up to a year.

If you have too many mange tout simply put them in boiling water for a minute, drain, then place them on a baking tray and freeze. Once frozen just put them all in a freezer bag and take out for stir fries etc.

8. Make the Vegetables the Centre of Your Meal

Rather than thinking 'what dish shall I cook today?' instead see what is fresh and ready to pick and then build a meal around that. Every crop can be the star - cauliflowers make cauliflower cheese with parmesan croutons, potatoes make tartiflette (not very Greek, I know) and peppers and mange tout go into a lovely stir fry. We have a freezer full of halved, deseeded peppers to make stuffed peppers throughout the year.

9. Foraging

There are so many herbs and vegetables to forage. Thyme, sage and rosemary grows almost everywhere, as does wild fennel. Greeks tend to use the fennel leaves chopped up in salad rather than the bulb. Best of all is wild Mani asparagus, or '*sparaggi*'.

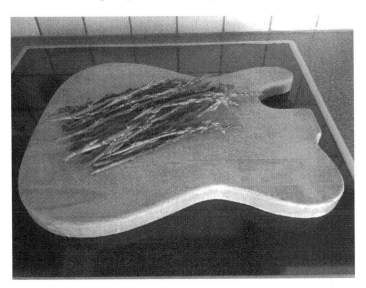

This grows on what looks like a rather nasty, thorny bush and is ready to pick around the end of February. Most people know the location of the plants, especially on main dog walking trails and so it gets picked almost immediately. But during the summer it is about the only bush to not go brown and its green colour stands out a mile. Make a note of the location of the more hidden bushes to revisit in February - it is very unlikely there will be any snakes at this time of year, they generally come out from hibernation at the end of March onwards.

10. Compost

As in the UK you will need some good compost. The very best comes from chicken poo, but it has to be broken down for about 9 months - if put on in its raw state it will kill the plants.

11. Watering Systems

For the first few years after we planted all our fruit trees I would water them just using a hose. It would take about half an hour, sometimes in the baking heat. There is a much easier and cheaper way - set up a watering system. This is basically just a long black hose attached to the tap with attachments that you fit at appropriate points where water comes out, essentially targeting the trees.

It's incredibly easy to set up and also very cheap. To do a whole field of 30 trees cost less than €50 and took a few hours. Start at the tap, and lay out the hose in the formation that you want it and at each tree using a special tool make a hole in the hose and attach a little black and red unit. This has a valve that allows you to control the amount of water that each tree gets, or you can even completely turn the water off at individual points. At the end of the hose fit a simple part that closes off the water.

Trust me, it is easier than I am making it sound - it's like playing with Lego or Meccano. Each day turn it on and return in 30 minutes to shut it off. It is such a time saver I kick myself for not putting in a system sooner.

You can even go one step further as I have and fit a timer so I don't even need to remember to water. These vary in cost and difficulty to use and are between €20 and €45.

12. Planting Trees

The previous owner of our house put in 20 or so trees and all but one died. Luckily I had local knowledge helping me and with the exception of two olive trees all mine have survived.

My friend told me that you had to dig a 1 metre cubed hole for each tree then fill the hole with water. Once this drains down, fill the bottom with the best compost you can get, put in the tree and then fill around with more compost. Each tree needs support from a metal pole to protect it from strong winds. If on an incline, put a circle of stones around the lower part and leave the top clear. This means water can drain in, but not out, so is trapped.

Chapter Fifteen: Floyd, My Second Best Friend in the World

As I previously mentioned, the last meal I had in the UK with my family was sat at the table where my hero, Keith Floyd sadly ate his last meal. I grew up with Border Collies from rescue homes and had always wanted another one. Perhaps subliminally I was trying to recreate my childhood, which was fantastically happy, I don't know.

Up until this point in my life however it just wasn't possible. Work was always too crazy for me to keep a dog; it just wouldn't have been fair. But now we owned our own house, no landlord, we worked from home and we had loads of land for a dog to run about in.

I looked for several years at the dogs that needed rehoming, but there were no Border Collies. One might argue that I should just adopt another dog and it is a fair point. But I had waited almost 30 years and I really, really wanted a Border Collie.

I found a reputable breeder in Thessaloniki who bred Border Collies and clearly adored his dogs. It went against my principles as I believe that there are so many animals looking for a good home that we really shouldn't be paying for a pedigree dog. Could I justify it because I had given so many cats a loving home? Perhaps partly, but really I'm not sure that it goes 100% of the way. OK, I admit it, I am a hypocrite. But this will be the only exception to the rule.

Thessaloniki, pronounced *Thess-a-lonn-eeki*, is in the far North East of Greece and Stoupa is in the far South West. Greece is a big country and to drive there would have taken us a little over nine hours. With the memory of having driven five hours with the cats from Athens still in the back of our minds, we looked into alternatives. We could fly from Kalamata to Thessaloniki, it was just a 45 minute flight and the airline allowed you to take animals of 4kg or less as 'hand luggage'.

We were worried about taking an animal on board a flight as neither of us had ever done it before, but there didn't seem like any other alternative. We were reassured on the flight up when we counted the passengers other than us numbered just four. Brilliant, if the flight back was the same we could find a spot away from everyone else if the dog played up.

If you haven't been to Thessaloniki, do - it really is an amazing place. We are both lucky enough to have travelled extensively around the world, but neither of us had seen anything like it. It is an amazing party town, much like Bangkok, or Brighton in the summer, but we arrived on a Sunday in October. Bars were heaving, music, parties, it was amazing. I remember saying to Anne 'wow, it's a Sunday, is it always this crazy?' and a chap behind me overheard and said 'yes, it is always like this'. There is no beach in the city centre, just a long three lane road with a promenade that leads to the impressive White Castle and the road is closed off every Sunday to allow people to go for a stroll. At any given time there must be thousands and thousands of coffees being consumed along that stretch.

The next day we drove half an hour out of town and met the puppy for the first time. It was love at first sight, she was so tiny! By now you will have hopefully realised that Anne and I name any animal how we would like. A female animal can often be given a male name and for ages I have wanted a dog called Floyd. The fact that she was female didn't stop us, but has led to a fair amount of confusion. For quite a while when asked I tried to explain in Greek, but to this day I can't remember what 'drunken chef' in Greek is. Often people would say 'Ah, Pink Floyd' and I just found it easier to say yes.

Luckily our Airbnb had marble floors as when we got back Floyd managed to poo in five different places. She had wailed all the way back, but really, if you had just been taken away from your parents and siblings and handed to two strangers, wouldn't you do the same? I know I would.

I was up almost every single hour that night and slept on the sofa with her. Anne came in at around 4am to give me a few hours of rest, but neither of us slept much. We walked Floyd in the main square and then made our way to the airport.

On the way 'home': Anne and Floyd, Departures, Thessaloniki Airport, October 2015

Hoping for a nice empty plane again, we went through security. Floyd peed on the floor as we embarked onto the plane, but we had come prepared with baby wipes and kitchen roll. There is a Greek Army garrison in Thessaloniki, as Greece still has national service. Unfortunately for us it must have been time for R&R, as the airport was swamped with soldiers. Even worse, many of them were heading for Kalamata. The plane was full, not a single seat spare.

I get incredibly irritated when I am flying and people just leave their children to scream and wail. However, any parent that tries to calm down a toddler always has my utmost sympathy - it must be an incredibly stressful time and I never complain. I often see the look of fear on their faces. Being child-free meant I have fortunately never been in that position until now.

As soon as we took off Floyd started wailing. I tried my best to comfort her, but the stewardess, who was right next to me, told me I had to leave her in her carry bag by my feet. I couldn't even put her on my lap and once we reached a certain altitude I couldn't even walk her up and down the plane, something that had calmed her down previously.

I desperately felt for her and I desperately felt for the other passengers, many of whom were looking back in anger; some of whom were undoubtedly trained killers. Thankfully the flight was brief and after a while I ignored the stewardess and got her out onto my lap to calm her down, but she must have screamed for 35 out of the 45 minute flight.

I wanted to use that imaginary power that I wish I had, especially when taking the cats to the vet - the ability to talk to animals and for them to understand: 'It will be alright, don't worry. You are going to an amazing home where you will be loved and treated like royalty'. As the plane disembarked I could feel sets of eyes on me, but it was amazing to see people that had previously wanted to kill me absolutely melt when they saw the source of their irritation. Floyd was a star, just a rather noisy one at present.

My childhood Collies were a year or so in age when we adopted them, I had never owned a puppy before and, boy, was I about to learn some lessons. The ease at which we integrated our street cats into the house was a stark contrast to a puppy. I won't lie, we all found it very, very difficult; not just Anne and I, but Floyd as well. We decided to keep her in our office overnight. People had suggested using a crate and a friend had lent us one, but I didn't like the idea of it.

She wailed throughout the entire night. I didn't think vocal cords could be put through that much torture. Luckily we don't have immediate neighbours, but I was worried about Floyd. The whole thing must have been terrible for her with the journey and the new house, not being around her siblings and getting used to the two of us, not to mention the cats.

I later learned that I should have slept in the office with her and I wish I had done. Animal guilt is a tough one: I always try and do the right thing, but sometimes my best is just not good enough.

We had heard about a chap, Nikos, who trained dogs for the Greek Air Force and who had a sideline in training domestic animals, so we got in touch. Over the course of ten hour long lessons he taught me a huge amount and Floyd's behaviour improved massively. That is the point, he explained - you have to train the owner as much as the dog. There is a hierarchy and I am Number One. The dog has to realise that, but this is taught not by giving treats and most definitely not with any shouting or worse; it is done by making the dog want to please you, Number One.

Nikos told me that it was important that I remain calm, that I am a good leader. He told me to imagine that I was a General in the war - what qualities would the soldiers want to make them look up to you? I needed to remain calm under pressure, to have a plan, to reward good behaviour and call out bad behaviour in the same way.

We walked long distances and talked lots, he was a lovely guy. He loved UK football, something that is very common out here, the UK league is much admired by the Greeks. Liverpool FC was his team - they seem a very popular team here - and he planned on getting a huge LFC sleeve tattoo on his right arm. He was also planning a trip to Anfield, only the second time he would have been abroad and he told me his route: Kalamata to London Heathrow.

'There is a much better route for you - you can fly direct from Kalamata to Manchester and there it is only a short drive to Liverpool'

'Yeah, I know, but that means stepping foot in *Manchester*'. He even knew the old British rivalries and told me that he had decided that his gravestone would read 'Yes, this is bad, but I could be in Old Trafford'.

Floyd's first walk off the lead was at a deserted beach. Greek law regarding dogs on beaches is strict: they are not allowed at all during holiday season of May to October. If you are caught you risk a fine and some, mainly older, Greeks get very upset. It is just not worth it. However, if you can find a deserted beach, and there are many around here, you are fine. I let her off the lead and immediately she ran for the sea and jumped in. It was the start of her love affair with water, one that continues to this day. I've never seen this before, but when she gets out instead of just shaking off the water, she does a huge dive and then a 'Snoopy Dance' on her back in the sand. She comes out absolutely covered in sand - surely that's not comfortable? Day after day I was learning what makes Floyd such a unique and gorgeous dog.

One of the other reasons for getting a puppy is that we were worried about how a dog would change the dynamics of a house with nine cats. After all, the cats were there first and the dog would have to fit in around them. We felt it was more likely to succeed with a puppy rather than an adult dog. As it turned out, Floyd was fine with all the cats. She perhaps wanted to be friends with them more than they wanted to be friends with her, but there was no trouble whatsoever with one perhaps easy to guess exception - Jeeves, Pringle Boy, Mr Taliban.

Jeeves absolutely *hated* having his position as the dominant animal in the house usurped by a new, bigger, stronger, growing imposter. Unfortunately, they hated each other equally and we saw the first of many scraps between them. It says something about Jeeves' character - I am not exactly sure *quite* what though - that he would even consider taking on an animal who, fully grown, was 22kg - almost four times his size. To this day, they still hate each other and we have to try and keep them apart, like a boxing referee. Feeding times are particularly tough. Hell, feeding ten or so animals in one room is an absolute nightmare and always will be.

There now follows something that I bet will be familiar to every single dog owner reading this: letting the puppy out to roam the house at night.

We didn't like keeping Floyd in the office at night. Anne's ruined desk and chair would attest to the fact that the office didn't like it much either. But now her puppy phase had passed it didn't feel right. We wanted her to have the run of the house, which had the added bonus of giving us some extra security.

Anne was not wholly convinced, but relented, saying 'OK, just not in the bedroom'.

The first night, Floyd played by the rules, but on the second morning we awoke to find her asleep on the floor next to me, her Number One.

'OK, we'll let her in the bedroom, just not on the bed'.

Two days later we woke up to find her on the bed, at the bottom next to two cats.

I loved her, everyone loved her. We met more people in the first two months of owning her than in five years of living here. Who doesn't love a Border Collie?

Another worry was how she would be with the chickens, but that worry was soon put to rest. She might not be the world's best herder, but we can lock her in the field with the hens, let them run free and know that she will protect them against any predators.

Her love of water extended to the swimming pool and she tried on several occasions to get in. Once I stupidly allowed her and we managed four lengths together before Anne caught us. Her herding instincts met with her love of water and she would run along as we swam lengths, doing one circuit of the pool for every length we did - 30m for every 10m we swam. In the summer we find this particularly useful, as to walk her in the extreme heat is too much for us and for her as well, the ground is too hot for her paw pads and there is no shade from any trees, as olive trees barely grow more than 3m in height here. A 45 minute swim for us with her herding us is more than enough exercise for her and for us. There then follows a familiar and predictable routine. We finish the swim and get out, she runs down to the deepest part of the overflow to cool down, sits there for 2-3 minutes, gets out, 'Snoopy Dances' on her back in the gravel, 'Snoopy Dances' on her back in the mud under the olive tree, back to us … in an absolutely shocking state.

In the winter one of our favourite things to do is to go on hikes up in the mountains. There are several circular walks we do, often along *kalderimis*, or raised stone goat trails, through mountain villages. Another favourite route starts and ends in Kardamyli and takes in Agios Sofia and Proastio via the most amazing church. It doesn't look much from the outside, but inside has stunning religious paintings; truly breathtaking.

It was on this walk that we discovered another amusing trait - Floyd is scared of sheep. Yes, my adorable hound was absolutely petrified when confronted by the very animal that her predecessors were famous for, and excelled in, controlling.

Now, aged six, she is the most loving, loyal and friendly animal I have ever met. As I type she is at my feet, in fact I estimate that since we got her she has spent 98% of her time within a two metre distance of me; she is my companion and my shadow, my second best friend in the world.

One thing I remember about Collies from my childhood is their absolute love of cars and Floyd is no different. She will insist on coming along to every journey - even a trip to the supermarket. She gets to go in the car, then I tie her up in the shade outside the supermarket where she gets loads of attention, and then back up the mountain in the car. Luckily our car is not an expensive make or model, as she insists on sitting in the passenger seat with the window down, then she pokes her head out, using the wing mirror as a perch for her paws, tongue out, drooling, ecstatic. The passenger door is completely scratched up from these numerous journeys down and back up the mountain.

Chapter Sixteen: The Good Things About Greece; An Occasional List

Five years in a country is a good enough time period to reflect on what is good and what is bad about it and I love lists, so in no particular order, here are the things I love about Greece, followed in the next chapter by the things I am less enamoured with.

1. The Weather

Greece is a huge country and the weather varies massively. There is quite often snow in Northern Greece, but down here in the Mani, which is about as far South West as you can go on the mainland, I've never seen it, other than from afar on the mountains. The Mani often has some of the best weather in the country.

Winter starts around November, but it is often well into the 20s in December. January and February are traditionally cooler, down to 12 degrees or so when the rains come. Despite spending a lot of time in South East Asian monsoons, I have never seen rain quite like it. It is much needed and it really doesn't mess around when it arrives. Every now and again, Mother Nature reminds you exactly who is boss. I've seen over 100 km/h winds, twisters coming in from the sea, hail and the biggest lightning storms ever. You have to disconnect any modems during the lightning, as a hit will blow the thing to pieces. In our first house before we had worked this out we took a direct hit and the modem flew a metre in the air in a puff of acrid smoke. This has happened on multiple occasions since.

By March, things are generally drier, and the gorgeous wild flowers come out everywhere. April is when the heat really gets up and normally one day in April it just switches from 'nice and warm' to summer. There comes a time in March/April where you know that you will have 7-8 months of fantastic weather and as an Englishman I can't begin to describe what a wonderful feeling that is. Even if rain comes it is welcome, as it often resets the temperature a few degrees lower, plus it is good for the garden.

People swim in the sea all year round, but personally I like it from May to October.

August and a fortnight either side can be brutal, sometimes more than 40 degrees - way too hot for me. It is also the period where Athenians come down on holiday, so the tavernas are packed, driving is terrible, roads are congested, so we just stay up here on the mountainside. It's a great time for local business owners and no one can begrudge them that, their work ethic is astounding, but we just prefer to stay out of the mayhem.

September and October are lovely, the heat subsides, it's quieter and even though the chance of rain and storms increase, they are both very enjoyable months. You don't normally need a jumper on if you are eating out at night.

2. The Mani Is an All Year Round Place

Of course, people come here for the sun and the sea, but there is so much more to do than just sunbathe and swim. From October to March the hiking is amazing, a lot of trails up in the mountains that are properly mapped out - plus a few that take you all the way up to the top and then the markings suddenly end. You can take trails up to a number of mountain villages, get a nice taverna lunch and then make your way slowly down with full bellies. The majority of hikes we do are in the 3-4 hour range - much longer is beyond us!

Just 2.5 hours' drive north through Kalamata and towards Tripoli is the village of Kalavrita, a winter ski resort. Despite having my snowboard and boots and all of the rest of my gear in the loft I am ashamed to say I have never been. My previous knee and ankle injury has made me more wary with my advancing years, but I am determined this will have to be remedied next season.

3. The People

I adore the Greek people, or perhaps more accurately I should say that I adore the people that live around here, because there are people of many nationalities. Some of my best friends are Greek and Albanian - there is a large Albanian population here - but just down my road we have Greek, English, German, French, Albanian and Swedish.

One of the Greek traits is a little bit of craziness and I mean that in a loving way. They are not massive fans of authority and the area is still somewhat lawless, but, again, in a good way. People respect each other, the police are rarely seen or needed. Gun ownership is incredibly high, in fact there are shotgun cartridges and magnum bullets on sale in the local supermarket on a shelf that is ankle high, right next to the cat food.

Guns are regularly fired during Easter and I am told that once a man got a bit excited at a wedding and fired his AK-47 into the air.

4. The Food and Drink

Later on I will share with you the recipes for my takes on Greek classics. Greek food is absolutely wonderful - steeped in history, but also simple in many cases, making the most out of fresh, seasonal ingredients. It is generally not complex or multi-layered, like French or Chinese, but I would argue that its simplicity, freshness and use of local ingredients are the key.

Food is incredibly important to Greeks. It is a time for family to come together and share, often incredibly late into the night and the next morning. Greeks love to drink too, but are far more restrained than us Brits. Quite often you can walk along the sea front at lunchtime and see table after table of people drinking beers and then a table of people drinking coffees. It is a fair bet that the tables with beer on are Brits or Germans and the coffees are for the Greeks.

Greeks are *obsessed* with coffee. There is a large electrical shop in Athens that we go to sometimes and I would estimate that 25% of the floor space is given away to coffee machines; a quarter of the shop, just filled with every kind of coffee machine you could imagine.

I'll skip quickly through the drinks as I am sure you already know most of them.

The house wine served is very drinkable. It is usually €3 per half litre, although one taverna gives a half litre away free per couple with food - they give out a card for life with this pledge.

Of the beers, Mythos is probably the best known, but my favourite is Fix, the oldest Hellenic beer.

The most famous spirit is Ouzo, an aniseed flavoured drink often added to water. I think it is fair to say that it is not for me. Then there is Metaxa, Greek brandy. Anne stopped me from drinking Metaxa, even the seven starred stuff, as she said I smelled like a tramp. Charming.

To the food; I have tried to replicate many of these dishes at home and in the Appendix you will find my recipes, with my take on those dishes marked with an asterisk. This is by no means an exhaustive list, just a few particular favourites:

Kleftiko*. This is an absolute favourite of mine. I hope to spend the rest of our lives in Greece, but if we were forced to move, this is the dish I would miss the most. Its name roughly translates as 'Bandit Lamb', as originally a sheep would be stolen from a nearby flock and the lamb cooked in a clay pot dug into the ground with potatoes, vegetables , herbs some wine and olive oil for many hours.

'Kleft' is the stem for thief or robber ('Kleftis' - a word we would soon sadly get to learn) and is the basis for the English word 'Kleptomaniac'. Today the clay pot method has been replaced by greaseproof paper, but a good kleftiko will have a base of nice garlicy potatoes, then usually topped with slow cooked lamb - but pork and beef is also an option - tomatoes, carrots, onion etc. The final twist is melted cheese on the top. It is the ultimate comfort food.

Once, a favourite taverna of mine, one where I only ever ordered their kleftiko for many years, said to me 'would you like to try something different? Trust us'. I did trust them and later they brought out a fine looking dish, if somewhat familiar. They explained that they had a customer the previous week who, on seeing the browned greaseproof paper of his kleftiko, thought that it was part of the dish and tried to eat it, so it gave them an idea and they wanted a kleftiko addict/connoisseur to try it out. Instead of the greaseproof paper they wrapped the usual ingredients in filo pastry and cooked it until golden - an edible wrapping! It was gorgeous and possibly made me the first person in Greece to ever eat a kleftiko pie. I'll say those magical words again: Kleftiko. Pie.

Gyros*. This is the King of Greek street food - unbelievably tasty and a very cheap way to eat, with most costing between €2-€2.5. One is easily enough, two is even better. The correct pronunciation for this fantastic feast is similar to the English word 'Hero'. Rolled up in a round, warmed pita is firstly a good few spoons of tzatziki, then the gyros meat, which is spiced pork or chicken. On top of that is raw red onion, tomato and then some piping hot chips. Finally a shake of paprika, roll it up and there you have it. *Telio* ('perfect'). This snack is also the source of some of our terrible music puns, such as 'I'm Bonnie Tyler' ('Holdin' Out for a Gyros') and once I have had three, my listening tastes move to The Stranglers ('No More Gyros Any More').

Pastitsio*. This is similar to a lasagne and like many dishes in Greece varies from taverna to taverna. It is lighter than a lasagne and delicately spiced with bay, cinnamon and nutmeg. The lightness comes from adding egg yolk into the béchamel at the end. The bottom of three layers is pasta and the type differs from place to place. I have seen penne and even just normal spaghetti, but normally smaller, tubular pasta is used, similar to ditalini. Next is a layer of what is effectively ragu - mince with onions, tomato sauce cooked in wine and herbs. The final layer is the light béchamel. I have seen the overall servings come to over 4 inches in height, wobbling on the plate.

Souvlaki*. Souvlaki is a classic Greek dish that many British people will know and is effectively cubed, marinated meat on a stick then BBQ'd. I have had chicken, pork and lamb souvlaki in Stoupa. Often the meat will be divided by onion and pepper. To get the right taste, neck meat is often used as it has the right fat content. A neat trick was shown to me by a friend who said to get the very best tasting meat, marinate it overnight in a freezer bag with olive oil, garlic, white wine, oregano and thyme. This means you don't need to constantly turn each individual stick. Serve with piping hot chips and a big slice of lemon and that is just Greece on a plate.

Kolokythes Keftades (Fried Courgette Balls)* I absolutely love these as a starter and they are easy to make. Along with grated courgette is grated carrot, tomato and some potato, together with a handful of herbs, mainly mint. At home I serve them with a Greek yoghurt and lemon dip (lemon juice and zest), but in restaurants they usually just come on their own.

Saganaki/Garides Saganaki I've put these two together as they have a similar name, but they are in fact two very different things. Saganaki itself is a slab of cheese (usually kasseri), dipped in a light batter and fried, served with a nice big slice of lemon. Salty, fried cheese! *Garides Saganaki*, however, is shrimps served in a rich tomato sauce with Feta and a dash of ouzo. Please don't let the ouzo put you off; I am not the biggest ouzo fan myself, but it is that dash that makes the dish. I had eaten it numerous times and just couldn't quite make out what the mystery ingredient was, so I asked a waiter and he let me in on the secret.

Beef Stifado. Beef stew with a lovely thick tomato, wine and herb sauce, with lots of small, 'stifado' onions.

Briam* This is usually a side dish, but works perfectly as a standalone and is oven baked vegetables. Many Greeks say that it should really just contain potato and courgette, but this of course varies. My take on it has many more ingredients, including one or two secret ones that make the dish, the source of which was my best Greek friend here, as her mother makes it.

Spetsofai*. Another favourite to have in tavernas or at home, spetsofai uses loukanika, or spiced mountain sausages, often with orange in, grilled and sliced then added to a spicy tomato sauce with onions and pepper. Serve with lots of crumbled Feta on top.

5. Stray Kittens

Animals make a place, in my opinion. There are far fewer strays here now than when we first arrived. None of the originals have survived, but these reduced numbers have more to do with the efforts of the animal welfare groups and the many volunteers, plus the work of Kostas the vet.

The vast majority of tavernas allow stray cats in. Some don't and I can completely understand their views on this, as there are obviously many diners who just want to be left alone while eating. But almost all of the cats keep a respectable distance and to me, a meal isn't an experience without the sea, the company, the food and - of course - the stray cats.

Some of our best memories of Stoupa bay are from nice warm winter days, walking along the bay with Floyd and feeding the stray cat crew. There are often a few sun loungers left out and about during the off season and it is not unusual for us to lie back on one and be joined by four strays each for an hour or two. Perfect.

6. The Smell

After our first trip to Kefalonia it wasn't the sun, the sea, the food or the people that was my most vivid memory - it was the smell. We used to go in early July and by that time it is really heating up. Summer in Greece for me is defined by the smell. It is a mixture of citrus, burned herbs and pine.

But living in Greece year round means you get to enjoy my other favourite smell: burning olive logs. During the olive harvest a fair few logs are cut when pruning the tree and these are left to season over the summer in a store that usually has cover from the rain, but also allows air flow through the sides. In the evenings in late October onwards, the logs are put to use heating houses and the sweet smell of burning olive logs is just wonderful.

7. There Is Beautiful Colour All Year Around

Back in the UK I used to find winters incredibly depressing. They can get cold and are sometimes very wet in Greece too, but there is one saving grace other than the smell of burning olive; there is always colour. Firstly, olive trees don't lose their leaves and after very strong winds they often show the underside of their leaves, which are a beautiful silver colour. From February to April the wild flowers come out, of all different colours, together with some orchids. This is our field last spring.

The field in spring. Spot the cat!

They tend to follow a similar pattern every year: first come the yellow flowers, then white, then pink, then finally the red.

Bougainvillea brings intense red colour and flowers much of the year and there is also huge amounts of Oleander, with white, pink or red flowers. This last flower is as beautiful as it is dangerous, as all parts of the plant are toxic and can kill if ingested. It should not be burned inside either. There are apocryphal stories of Roman legions camping near Oleander and using their long, straight branches as skewers for cooking meat, with terrible consequences.

Lastly, most orange and lemon trees are fully laden with ripening fruit by November time and the fruit often remains well into February or even longer. It is a strange thing at first to see a tree absolutely groaning with oranges with a snow capped mountain behind it, but it is a favourite winter view now.

8. Eating and Drinking out is Cheap

In fact it is really, really cheap Starters at a taverna range between €2-€5 and mains around €7-€12, although prime steaks and fish are more expensive. An ice cold 500l draft beer is between €2.50-€3.50 and house wine is €3.50 for 500l and as previously mentioned, one taverna even gives it away for free with food. It's very drinkable, there is no need to buy 'proper' bottles of wine unless you want to. Many tavernas will give you a small free dessert, such as cake, a plate of fruit, yoghurt and honey, cheesecake, or my favourites, louakoumades, which are like hot mini dough balls, usually served with ice cream or yoghurt and honey, plus crushed nuts.

All in, it is very easy for a couple to eat out with starters and main courses, 500ml of wine and probably a free dessert for a little less than €30. If there are more of you than two, or if you wish to have a selection of starters - meze - it can come in even cheaper.

And the best thing of all? Prices have not changed in the slightest in the ten years we have been here from 2010. Compare all of that with the UK!

Tipping is a difficult topic around the world as amounts expected vary. I know of someone who was almost chased out of a restaurant in the US for giving a tip of 19.8%. When we first arrived, tipping wasn't all that common, but we have always given around 10% as wages here are low and we like to show appreciation for a lovely meal and service. Once when I gave 15% and they brought the bill back to me and said I had made a mistake!

Whilst eating and drinking out is wonderful value, the cost of food at the supermarket is actually quite high - Waitrose prices. White goods are very expensive too, while utilities are broadly in line with the UK.

9. The Medical System is Wonderful

Greece has been in the UK press headlines for its 'creaking' health system, but I'm sadly not sure if many systems around the world can sadly be described as tip-top these days. There is a public system, with a medical centre in Agios Nikolaos, just below us, for more minor ailments and a hospital in Kalamata for more serious afflictions. I have used both and been seen almost instantly. The medical centre was for a blood test and that was performed immediately. The hospital was for an x-ray on my injured foot and I was in and out in 45 minutes.

Obviously stories will vary depending on whom you speak to, but the general view is that the public system, around here at least, works pretty well.

On top of that you have the private system, which is thoroughly efficient and, compared with the UK, very cheap. We are also lucky to have the incredibly talented Dr Sofia in Stoupa village. She charges between €20 and €30 for a consultation. There is no waiting list, you just turn up and wait to be seen. It is best to avoid the first days of the months and also Mondays, but the longest I have ever waited to be seen is about 30 minutes.

As I am sure you will agree, when I am ill I just want to be seen right away, immediately, and in this part of Greece you can do so.

The village dentist saw me within 30 minutes after I called for an appointment in pain. Four individual sessions of root canal cost €160 in total.

We also have a Medical Lab on the road between Stoupa and Agios Nikolaos that carries out blood tests. Coincidentally, the main doctor there used to work at our nearest hospital in London, The Royal Free Hospital, and lived 1km from us in London before we moved here. For reasons you will read about later, I now have to have monthly blood tests - one sole item - but the cost to take the blood, analyse it and send it back to me via email the same day is €13, no appointment needed, normally no wait at all.

Should you need anything over and above what is on offer on our doorstep, Kalamata has a large number of specialists, largely situated on the first floor above retail units on two adjacent streets off the main square. A consultation is usually €50 and you are seen almost immediately.

Due to my mother's cancer, I have to be examined every five years, as the probability is that I will get cancer too. When I first looked into the tests in the UK, I was quoted around £1,500. I have to go private in the UK because whilst I still pay certain UK taxes as well as Greek tax, as I am no longer a UK resident I no longer qualify for NHS treatment. I told Dr Sofia and she put me in touch with a specialist in Kalamata. The cost? €150.

Whilst I am no medical specialist, the logic that the Greeks use makes perfect sense to me. If you have had an accident or have problems with your spine, leg, foot etc they send you for an MRI scan. The cost is approximately €100, but it means they can accurately pinpoint precisely what is wrong with you. If your ailment is of the 'non-physical' nature they send you for a blood test, which again means they can accurately diagnose your problem.

Anne used to experience severe back pain when we lived in the UK, meaning she had to either take time off work, sometimes weeks, or work from home. Here, she had an MRI and the follow up consultation showed a herniated disc. The consultant gave her tablets to take when she felt her back twinge and she has never had the problem again. It makes complete sense, but an MRI was never even offered in the UK. How can you accurately diagnose when you are blind to the issues?

It is no exaggeration to say that the Greek medical system saved my life, as I will later explain.

Chapter Seventeen: Downsides of Living in Greece

Whilst I hope this book reads like the love story about Greece I intended, it would not be right to omit the negatives about living here and, like everything, there are negatives. In no particular order:

1. Bureaucracy

Of course, bureaucracy exists the world over, but Greece takes it to new levels. Before you can do anything you need to get a tax code and for this you usually need a Greek sponsor. In our case our first landlord helped us out and vouched for us - if he hadn't helped I doubt we could have done it, naïve as we were back then.

The tax office in Kalamata is a chaotic building not far from the old port, bereft of any signs to tell you precisely which queue to join. Greeks aren't massive fans of queuing either, but we managed to get our tax numbers within around half an hour. You need your tax number for so many things - in fact, life without one in Greece would almost be impossible. For example you can't get a landline or electricity without one, nor can you buy a house.

You will often get asked for your passport too, for example when you buy a mobile phone. And you will often be asked for your father's name to go on official documents. A neighbour in his 80s was once asked for his mother's birth certificate, when she had passed away 30 years previously.

Perhaps the most extreme form of bureaucracy came when a friend's son was selected to play for his junior school's football team. His mother had to produce his original birth certificate before he could play at every single game - they would not take a copy and assume that as he was available to play he was still alive.

We've pretty much come to the conclusion that if we need to anything official we need to take a bundle of documents: passport, tax number, residency card, driving licence, tax number, utility bill, deeds to the house, marriage certificate. Not all will be needed of course, but you can bet that the day you don't bring something is the day you are asked for it.

2. Driving

I thought that London drivers were bad. Greek drivers are in a different league, almost fearless, in an environment of blind bends and sheer 200 ft drops.

I remember when I was young and we got our first dog, Thea, and I'd walk her with friends and their dogs. Thea *always* had to be the dog in the lead, the one nearest the park, and she reminds me of Greek drivers. They cannot stand to be behind you and will take crazy risks just to get ahead, even if you are going at a fair pace.

I've lost count of the accidents I have witnessed and the small roadside shrines, *kandylakia*, are testament to lives lost. These often very well maintained concrete or metal boxes are dotted along the route to Kalamata.

That journey, about an hour, taking in sea, mountain roads and coastal routes would be absolutely amazing on a nice powerful motorbike, but I just won't risk it.

3. 'Avrio'

If you looked the word *'avrio'* up in the dictionary it would tell you that in English it means 'tomorrow'. It doesn't. If a builder or other workman tells you 'avrio' it actually means 'tomorrow … or any day *after* tomorrow'. It can be days or weeks after.

4. Crime

Whilst absolutely nothing on the scale of London, there is still crime here. I've not heard of any serious crime, such as murder or assault however, it tends to be 'just' theft and break-ins.

One day early on in our time here there was an audacious crime against our lovely, now late, postman, Stavros. On the bend near

Foneas beach, just outside Stoupa, a gang staged a bike accident with the intention of getting Stavros to stop his car. It was pension day and often pensions are paid in cash. Stavros didn't stop and they fired several shots at him before staging an armed robbery at a bank on the outskirts of Stoupa.

I should point out that this was a one-off and as a repeated victim of crime back in London as I mentioned before, it is a lovely sight to walk along Stoupa bay and see scooter after scooter with the keys left in and the helmet on the seat. Crime does still exist, but it is thankfully rare.

5. Animal Cruelty

Sadly, like crime, this exists too. Thankfully, too, it is very rare and almost exclusively carried out by the older generation. The youngsters are being educated on animal welfare and now understand perfectly well that it is not acceptable and so hopefully this will become a thing of the past, where it belongs.

6. Extreme Weather

I adore the climate here and the changing seasons. There is something beautiful about every season and I don't think I could live somewhere like the Caribbean where there is no winter. That said, I have never seen such extreme weather anywhere else in the world. When it rains it can wash cars into the sea, such is its ferocity. When the wind gets up I have seen it so strong that my greenhouse once flew past my window. Stoupa is in an earthquake zone, as the Kalamata quake of 1986 shows, but all new houses and pools are built to stringent earthquake regulations. I can only remember two quakes in a decade here and they were relatively minor.

7. Greece is Still a Patriarchy

It is a man's world. Sunday morning down at the fishing village below us is packed with men drinking coffee, smoking, putting the world to rights, barely a single woman amongst them.

This male dominance can have strange outcomes, however. For example, historically, the son generally was the beneficiary of the best land, with the daughter getting the inferior land as an inheritance. Until recently, the 'best' land was the fertile land in the mountains where you could grow olives and the 'inferior' land was the coastal land with poor soil near the beaches. The arrival of tourism in the 1990s turned things on its head and meant that often the 'inferior' inheritance became the most valuable!

8. Property Law

This is an area where over time I've learned a lot and yet the more you learn, the harder it gets and the more you realise you don't know. Greece doesn't yet have a centralised land registry. The EU gave them the funds to create one and when they inspected the offices, found about 200 people - bizarrely mostly former hairdressers - twiddling their thumbs.

Property rights are a tough area too, with often competing claims on the same land. In his book 'Blue Skies and Black Olives', former BBC journalist John Humphreys tells the story of a man who bought a plot of land only to find the former owner harvesting the olives from the trees several months later.

'Excuse me, this is my land now'.

'Oh yes, it is your land, but the trees are still mine'.

There is also the issue with Forestry land, which cannot be built on, but it often takes many months to get a certificate to prove the land isn't classed as Forestry - ours took five months. In recent years, the authorities have been reclassifying land as 'Forestry', meaning that if your house already existed on it you had to pay more tax. Greeks saw through this as a rather cynical way to increase the tax take. When the Forestry team arrived here, they received a local 'welcome': their car was pelted with eggs.

As I previously mentioned there is the 800m rule, which states that within an 800m radius of the village church you can generally build what you like, but outside that you need a plot of 4,000m^2 to build. We had several GPS reports carried out and they said we were at the very edge of the radius. In fact, if our house went 10cm further south it would have had to be completely demolished and I know of several houses in the area that have met that fate. Imagine building a house and then having to pay for it to be knocked down.

9. Bribery, '*Fakelaki*'

Much is made in the UK press about bribery in Greece, or '*fakelaki*', meaning little envelopes, often purported to be given to jump waiting lists for operations, or to get planning permission. I have never seen it. I thought at one time during our planning process that the officers were holding out for a bribe, indeed as I said earlier, I asked my architect, but she said they normally take a long time to make a planning decision and that bribery is rarely seen any more.

A friend once gave a doctor who had operated on her brother some money to buy a bottle of wine, to say thank you and he gave it back thinking he was being bribed. I'm not saying it doesn't go on, it must do as it does everywhere, I just haven't ever seen it, or been asked for a bribe.

Chapter Eighteen: 2016, Annus Horribilis

So, 2016 ... where do I start? There are so many reasons why we didn't acquire any new cats that year.

I've thought long and hard about including this, but ultimately I decided to write about it for reasons of completeness and of honesty - it happened, much as I wish it hadn't. I will warn you, however: a lot of it is very dark.

I'd always known I was 'different' and by this I don't mean different in a positive way. I could never put it into words, but I just *knew*.

The year started with me struggling to get out of bed. In the past I had been prone to periods of depression and mania, mostly from about the age of 28. One day I was in such a bad way that I begged Anne to get Dr Sofia around, as she does house calls after her surgery. When she came I asked her for an injection just to put me to sleep for the day. She agreed, but before that we chatted about how I was feeling in general. Sofia is an internist. Internal medicine physicians, or internists, are specialists who apply scientific knowledge and clinical expertise to the diagnosis, treatment, and care across the spectrum from health to complex illnesses. We talked about my up and down moods and she noticed psoriasis on my elbows - a sign of stress. Before giving me my injection she recommended I go and see a specialist doctor in Kalamata and gave me his details.

The doctor asked me lots of questions about depression and mania, dangerous behaviour and also whether I spent large sums of money at any one time. I had to laugh then, as I was wearing shorts and a T-shirt that I had bought for £5 each from eBay and sandals that cost me €6 from Lidl. He laughed and said he had to ask, then said that one of his patients spent €20,000 in a casino that weekend just gone and a further €5,000 on a piece of art. Another had bought a goat in a manic state.

At the end of the hour he said words that would change my life forever: 'My diagnosis is that you have Bipolar 2'. I was 42 and this meant a severe change of lifestyle. I would have to take Lithium and antidepressants for the rest of my life and attempt to give up alcohol.

Lithium is one of the oldest stabilisers used to treat Bipolar, previously known as manic depression. It is one of the most effective too, but also very dangerous. If it goes wrong in terms of the level in the bloodstream, it can ruin internal organs, primarily the liver and kidneys, meaning dialysis for life, or even death. For that reason I had to start having my blood tested every three months, and this increased to every month during the summer, due to the heat causing dehydration.

I knew a fair bit about the subject before the meeting, as some of my musical heroes were Bipolar. Jimi Hendrix wrote 'Manic Depression' about it and Kurt Cobain wrote 'Lithium'. Historians believe Vincent van Gogh was Bipolar, as was Winston Churchill. Effectively, Bipolar is waking up one day not knowing if you are going to be Eeyore or Tigger. The mania was great, a lot of fun, the depression almost unbearable. I am lucky in life to have many passions; things that I love to do that interest me. I love to cook, swim, grow my own vegetables, keep chickens, walk my dog, listen to and read about music, I love chatting and just hanging out with Anne, I love art and I love our many animals. I am lucky. At times though, Bipolar robs you of all of that. When bad, I literally had no interest whatsoever in any of them and it feels like the smallest, most simple of tasks is beyond me. I remember describing it to numerous doctors as feeling like I had no skeleton, like I was walking through treacle.

Perhaps a more accurate, almost perfect, description of Bipolar comes from Kay Redfield Jamison:

There is a particular kind of pain, elation, loneliness and terror involved in this kind of madness. When you're high it is tremendous. The ideas and feelings are fast and frequent like shooting stars and you follow them until you find better and brighter ones. Shyness goes, the right words and gestures are suddenly there, the power to captivate others a felt certainty. There are interests found in uninteresting people. Sensuality is persuasive and the desire to seduce and be seduced irresistible. Feelings of ease, intensity, power, well-being, financial omnipotence and euphoria pervade one's marrow. But somewhere this changes. The fast ideas are far too fast and there are far too many; overwhelming confusion replaces clarity. Memory goes. Humour and absorption on friends' faces are replaced by fear and concern. Everything previously moving with the grain is now against - you are irritable, angry, frightened, uncontrollable and enmeshed totally in the blackest caves of the mind. You never knew those caves were there. It will never end, for madness carves its own reality'.

Walking out of the surgery, I felt strangely relaxed about such a bombshell. It certainly explained many things, not that I was looking for an excuse. I rang my parents to tell them and they said 'we know. With your brother we have been trying to find a diplomatic way to suggest that you should see a Bipolar specialist for some time'.

To nicer topics, albeit for just two paragraphs:

Back at home the pool was finally completed and it looked amazing. That first swim made everything seem worthwhile. The water was about an inch away from the top and I was sitting out with my iPad when an email from an old colleague came in. He wondered whether I would like my old job back! I looked around me and after maybe 30 whole seconds I politely declined. There was no way I could leave Greece. Working with that team again would have been a lot of fun and the company were the best employer I had ever had. But no, we had come too far down this route, I couldn't leave.

I got a reply a few minutes later: 'How about you take the job, but do it from Greece?' This offer was a lot harder to decline. It would mean a lot of travel however, and I just couldn't face the idea of being away from Anne and the animals. I thought long and hard, but eventually declined. Our life was now in Greece and this was where I wanted to stay.

It was early June and an important event loomed. I've thought long and hard about mentioning 'The B Word', Brexit, but really I *have* to include it, divisive as it is, and knowing that some people reading this book will heartily disagree with my viewpoint.

I am a staunch Remainer. I was before the referendum and I still am to this day. There is not one thing that has happened since the referendum that has made me question my view, but a huge amount of things that have happened that have reinforced my beliefs. Nothing whatsoever has changed my mind.

Of course I am a Remainer - I live in Greece courtesy of the EU's Freedom of Movement policy. I am also, for my sins, a qualified economist of 25 years' standing. Brexit makes absolutely no economic sense to me whatsoever and the non-economic arguments make just as little sense.

The world is changing and there are three economic powerhouse blocs that will shape this change, in different ways. Firstly there is America, the world's largest economy, for now. Even though it is in relative decline it will still be important in my lifetime. Then there is China, a country so vast and populated and so determined to dominate. Soon it will. Whilst we should take their growth figures with a pinch of salt, there is no doubt in which way it is heading. Lastly, there is the Eurozone. Whilst America is in slow decline and China is on the ascent, I would say the Eurozone is largely stable and will remain incredibly powerful.

Trade deals hinge on one thing: the strength and size of your economy. If Switzerland wants a trade deal with China, there will only be one 'winner', as indeed there was recently. It really is that simple, although not if you believe certain British politicians. To leave an albeit somewhat troubled economic powerhouse of 465 million people and branch out on our own with a mere 67 million people is sheer lunacy. As part of the EU we could dictate terms to others. Now the terms will be dictated to us. We are not taking back control, we are ceding it.

You would think that as people living in a foreign country by dint of a policy made by the EU that most British immigrants out here (I don't like the word *'expat'*) would also be Remainers, but you would be wrong. I estimate maybe well over half of the British people who live here voted Leave. How? Why? Many people I know couldn't vote however, because of the law that says that if you have left the UK for 15 years or more you have no vote. This goes for Brexit as well as Local Authority and also general elections. I'll repeat that: there is a referendum, the results of which will hit people living outside of the UK far more than those living in the UK. Many of these people have paid UK tax all their working lives or still are paying some form of UK tax and yet they get no say in their own future whatsoever; completely disenfranchised. How is that democracy?

I see many parallels between Brexit and the thing that got me first into politics at the late age of 29 - The Iraq War. The Iraq War had the support of both of the major political parties, as did Brexit. Public support for the Iraq War was over 60% before the war started, yet there were huge demonstrations in London and around the country by people like me who could see it was an action based upon lies. Like the Iraq War, Brexit had a majority, albeit a slim one. A million people peacefully marched against Brexit, also to no avail.

Yet after the disastrous war in Iraq, only 30% of the British public thought it was a good idea and I'll bet the same thing happens with Brexit.

The currency was hit badly. Given our earnings were in Sterling and our expenses were in Euros, that was an effective 25% pay cut. Since then things have improved slightly, the Pound trading in a range of €1.10-€1.20; still a very poor rate.

Worse was yet to come. People incredibly close to me inexplicably told me very firmly that they would also vote Leave.

As the Referendum day drew near I watched the odds at the bookies. I don't like opinion polls; they are subject to too much bias. If you look at where people are actually placing their money, rather than answering a survey, I find it often gets you closer to the actual end result. The bookies were saying it was close, but Remain would win … but a week before the result it switched into a slim win for the Leave camp. Even with my rule of trusting the bookies, I still refused to believe this could happen. I told a friend on my dog walk who was worried about the currency 'don't worry - if Remain wins it will bounce back to €1.45 as it was a month ago'.

I woke up at 3am on 24th June 2016 to hear the news. Devastated.

I decided to go for a long walk, or rather more accurately, a march, or a stomp, with Floyd. I couldn't believe this was happening. What would it mean for our life in Greece? I didn't believe what we were being told by the politicians, and it turns out I was right not to believe them. It would only be in April 2019 that things would become clear for us and we would feel secure. I'd already had my world turned upside down by the banking crisis - something I had absolute no control over - and now it could be happening once again.

About 10 minutes into my walk I bumped into a British neighbour, whom I shall not name. He told me he was selling his house after 15 years in Greece. I said that the vote yesterday might make things harder, given that Brits are amongst the most active house buyers in the area. He said 'yes, you're probably right, but I voted Leave anyway'.

WHAT!?

I asked his reasoning and he said that there were too many Lithuanian builders in his home town in the UK 'stealing' all the building work. His profession for a decade and a half in Greece? Yep, you guessed it: a builder. I previously had a lot of time for this chap, we had some interesting chats and he did some good work on our house, even if he did 'steal' that particular work from a Greek.

That very same day, 24th June 2016, we noticed that Marley was in pain and was having problems breathing. We called our vet, explained the symptoms and he recommended that we take her to another vet in Kalamata who specialised in animal heart problems. He saw us immediately and we waited three hours while he performed all sorts of tests. He said she was suffering from a heart condition called myocardiopathy. In layman's terms, it was a heart problem that meant liquid was being created, which restricts the heart pumping and reduces the capacity to breathe. She was basically drowning internally. He had to perform an emergency operation where he inserted a syringe into her thorax to drain the liquid, a nasty, blood coloured solution. About 150ml came out. He recommended an overnight stay for her and said that he would be checking on her at 3am, 6am and 9am.

The total cost for this treatment came to €250. I hate to think how much it would have been in the UK, well over £1,000 for sure.

We left Marls there in his capable hands and started the hour long drive up and over the Taygetos Mountains, exhausted, arriving home at 2am.

We spent the next day - our wedding anniversary - collecting her and making sure she was OK. The vet asked us how old she was and we couldn't answer as we got her as a stray from Archway Cat Rescue

Centre. She'd been with us for 13 years, so maybe 14 or 15? He told us to give her a tablet a day for the rest of her life, which he estimated would be only another six months. Thankfully he was wrong about that!

So, I was a mess, rapidly spiralling downwards. A combination of Bipolar, my diagnosis, money worries due to the weak Pound, Brexit, Marley's illness and the complete uncertainty about our future were dragging me lower and lower. On top of that, we had the stress of the long drawn out process of our swimming pool build, but really, that is the very definition of a first world problem.

I had already once lost a business and a life that I had worked so hard to build up and was proud of. It was completely out of my hands, I was powerless to influence any part of it, I just sat back and watched it crumble.

We came to Greece to escape all of that and had worked tirelessly to build a new life. Now was that going to be taken away as well? I speak to friends back in the UK and they have often said 'what is there to worry about? Everything is going to be OK', but that was simply not true. We were kept in the dark by our government for years, given no information about our futures. This uncertainty only ended on 9th April 2019, when the British Ambassador to Greece came to give a talk in Kardamyli. She was extremely impressive and we left knowing precisely what we would need to do to continue to remain living here. You should note the date however - almost three years after the referendum and nine days after we were actually originally meant to have left the EU. It is a long time to live in limbo.

I am ashamed of my behaviour at that time. I was out of control, near rock bottom. I was arguing with Anne - we hardly ever argue - I was angry with myself and the world, and I was drinking more than I should; much more.

It all came to a head one night in mid-August. I stormed out of the house, drove down to Stoupa and booked into a hotel. I just couldn't see a way forward. Yes, it really was that bad. I ate a meal then drank a bar dry of whisky, staying for so long that in the end they had to shut and gave me another double on the house as they left. I didn't know it, but there were several good friends down there in various different tavernas and bars who contacted Anne and said they were worried about me, who kept tabs on me and ensured Anne remained informed.

I got home the next day and Anne was frantic with worry. As I slumped on the sofa she said she had spoken to experts, done some research and found a psychiatric hospital in Athens with a place for me whenever I needed it.. Initially I resisted, but not for long. Deep down I knew I had reached a destination - Rock Bottom, population: me.

Anne drove us four hours to Athens, Kifissia to be precise, which seemed like a lovely, leafy northern suburb, not that I saw much of it or remember much of it.

We walked in and were told to go to the Head Doctor's office. I took an instant dislike to him; he talked to me like a pompous teacher to a pupil. I noticed that the window in his office was open and seriously contemplated jumping out of it. The fact that it was a first floor window - and I knew it was - should tell you the kind of state I was in. We discussed my issues and Anne went upstairs to check out the room. She said it was nice and that I should go. It was €200 a day plus medication. Before I went up they go through your bag to check for any items that are not permitted, such as alcohol and drugs. They took out my razors, belt, aftershave, shoe laces and even my large tea mug as someone could smash it and use it to slash their wrists

So ... this was my new home, a room at the far end of the corridor on the 3rd floor with a nice view over the lovely back gardens. It had a separate bathroom and shower, plus a personal smoking room. Only in Greece could you be in a hospital that has a smoking room! I kissed Anne goodbye and lay back on my bed.

A nurse came and gave me a handful of pills. I asked what they were, but she refused to tell me. She then fitted a cannula in my right hand to allow them to easily attach me to drips. This would remain in me throughout my stay, but wasn't all that much trouble.

For my first meal as a patient they brought me a lovely tray of pastitsio, salad, yoghurt and fruit. My Greek wasn't bad at this stage, so I asked the nurse for the wine list, thinking I was being funny. She didn't seem to think I was that funny.

Whatever drugs they gave me were very strong and I didn't react well to them at all. I was dizzy, completely out of it. I fell out of bed during the night and badly injured my knee. I shouted and shouted but no one came, so I tried to crawl along the corridor to get help. They found me about 20 yards from my room and helped me back.

I was in so much pain that they were worried about me as they said they would have to x-ray me. They brought a portable x-ray machine and photographed my knee as I lay in bed. They told me I had liquid on my knee that would cause arthritis and that there was only one way to get it out - needle and syringe. I had long got over my fear of needles, so I told them to go ahead. They took out three huge syringes of horrible brown liquid, the kind of stuff you would imagine to be in a smoker's lungs.

Meanwhile, four hours away, Anne was frantic. She was looking after 9 cats, 12 chickens and a puppy, all the time worrying about her useless (by my thinking, not hers) husband. Our neighbours heard about the situation and knocked on the door offering to walk Floyd. How lovely - we barely even knew them.

Things like that put our situation into perspective. We are thousands of miles away from our family and support network. How Anne coped I will never know. I am ashamed of what I put her through. Anne's parents were both elderly, her father was very ill and neither of them could travel at that time. I wasn't talking to my parents. Anne's sister was looking after their father. Other friends offered to come out, but it was a long journey for them, especially as most of them have families of their own to look after.

However, my super-busy, lovely brother dropped everything and came out from Switzerland to visit. We got Domino's pizza and walked around the garden to the basketball court. I picked the ball up in an effort to recreate the time when he and I had been in the winning team of the seniors' basketball competition at school, but only managed to throw it a pitiful four yards. I was a wreck.

I quickly fell into a routine:

Breakfast (three courses)

Drugs

Drip whilst in bed for three hours

Lunch (another three courses)

More drugs

Sleep

Dinner (3 courses)

Yet more drugs

Sleep

You'll notice each meal was three courses. In my stay there I put on two stone.

I rarely left my room or saw other patients, in fact I don't think I spoke to anyone other than the staff, who were all absolutely lovely. On the rare times I went out I had to take the lift down to the ground floor as I was too weak to go down or up the stairs.

The ground floor was heart breaking. These were long term patients, the vast majority of whom were never getting out. It really put my troubles into perspective, like some spoiled idiot in just for a rest. They were destined to stay in this 1,000m² compound for the rest of their days.

One of the three courses we got at mealtimes was a yoghurt, so three yoghurts a day. On my stroll around the grounds I saw lots of yoghurt cartons by a bush and looked in - a cat with kittens was being fed by the ground floor patients. There was also a wild tortoise in the garden. When the mother cat wanted to go off, on a few occasions the tortoise would come and look after the kittens. I'm glad I got a photo of this because I doubt anyone would ever believe me. I know I was on some very, very strong drugs, but here is the evidence.

Babysitter on the right, kittens on the left. .

Anne came to visit and it was so great to see her. She stayed the evenings in a hotel in Kifissia and would visit during the day, chatting with doctors. She was concerned with what they were giving me as I was so weak despite nine courses of food a day; I was like a zombie.

She insisted that the doctor come in and assess me. I don't remember any of this:

'What is your name?'

'Guy Hanley'

So far, so good.

'What year is it?'

'1975'

'O-kkkaaayyy ... who am I?'

'You', I said pointing at him, *'are ... Marty McFly!'*

It would have been funny if it were not so tragic. They agreed with Anne's judgement, changed my meds and I rapidly improved. As the days went by, I started to feel much better about everything and I decided that I would discharge myself, something I could do as I had entered the facility voluntarily.

I missed Anne, I missed my animals and I missed my mountain. Anne came up to collect me and to settle the bill - they don't let you out until you have paid the bill. It came to €6,000 - ouch! Never mind, I had medical insurance that would cover it. As I left they wished me well and told me I would have to start therapy or (in their words) *'we will be seeing you again'.*

Being home on my mountain was amazing, even though I was still in a bad, weakened state. A therapist in Kalamata was recommended and I started going to see her. The first time she politely told me to go home as she couldn't work with me in such a mess, but I soon was well enough to see her.

I don't want to be a therapy bore, but I found it to be a fantastic experience. It is slow moving, nothing happens in days or weeks, it is months or years. You think that you are going nowhere and then - BANG! - suddenly it hits you. Only then can you see precisely where it was all leading to. Perhaps the most useful was the theory of containment. Therapy doesn't try and eradicate things that have happened to you as to do so would be unrealistic - they *did* happen to you. Containment recognises that things have happened, but teaches you to deal with them in a more effective way. For example, imagine if you added a thimble of blue dye in a washing machine and switched it on - your clothes would all come out partly blue. But if you took that same thimble and placed it in an airtight container, put it in the wash and pressed the on button, your clothes would come out washed and in their original colour. The dye was present in both washes, but it only affected one set of washing. *That* in essence is containment and it still fascinates me to this day.

I ended up going to therapy for 18 months, weekly at first, then monthly, then every three months, then finally she told me that she thought I was ready to face the world. I took what the hospital in Athens said seriously, I was never even a minute late for my meetings and I never missed a single one. Actually, that last part is not true - I did miss one session, but that was with good reason. I was going to get better and I would never, ever sink as low as I had done that summer of 2016. Sometimes a stubborn nature can be a good thing. Sometimes.

So that was 2016 so far - an *annus horribilis*.

On 7th September 2016, a week after I was released from hospital, and still in a fairly bad way, the biggest storm in a quarter of a century hit Stoupa. I often say that out here, every once in a while, Mother Nature reminds you who is the boss. There was lightning, wind and lots and lots of rain. Four people sadly perished in Kalamata, trapped in a basement by incredibly fast rising water. Twelve cars got washed into the bay in Stoupa, three of them belonging to my neighbour's business. They had been parked on a run-off that doubles as a road, known locally as The Dragon and vast amounts of storm water cascaded down from the mountains, dragging them in. He also lost all of his tools when the van doors opened. As an experienced scuba diver he managed to retrieve most of them when things calmed down.

Closer to home, our modem blew (again) when we took a direct hit of lightning. The rain was so intense that we were cut off by fast flowing rivers across our road, meaning that I missed my therapy session for the first and only time. Looking out of my front door onto the once arid field next door there was so much fast flowing water I could have canoed down it.

The pool room of the just completed swimming pool quickly filled up to waist height, ruining approximately thousands of Euros worth of brand new heaters, filters etc. My newly built wall to extend the chicken run was smashed to pieces. It was utter devastation and I am ashamed to say I don't really remember much of it, much less help Anne, such was the state of my nascent recovery.

Are we still on 2016? Damn, it would appear so.

I've long hated insurance companies; they are a bunch of chiselling weasels. Many a time have I taken out a policy in good faith, paid the premiums and on the odd time I put in an honest claim they would find some reason to wriggle out of paying up.

Now, in 2016, their business model was under threat. What they used to do was take in the premiums, invest them and make a return. If they had to pay out they would have at least made some money in the meantime from investing your premium - that is why some of the biggest insurers also have some of the biggest bond trading operations in the UK.

But since the global financial crisis, with interest rates at near zero, they can't make a return on your premiums, so it appears that their business model now is 'take in the premium, then when an honest claim comes in, wriggle out of it somehow'.

We put in our claim for my hospital stay and learned a tough lesson about our Greek health insurance policy - it didn't cover mental health issues. They refused to pay the bill which was €6,000. Is mental illness any different to 'physical' illness? Because I sure *felt* ill.

We then put in our claim for the damage to the house and were certain that it would pay out because we explicitly went for cover to the house *and* the pool. That too was refused. This time they said 'well, yes, the pool itself is covered in your policy, but we specifically exclude pool rooms'. This was a UK company - it seems that insurance companies the world over are chiselling weasels.

That was an expensive week - somewhere around €20,000 of genuine insurance claims refused.

For Anne's birthday I was feeling incredibly sluggish, almost unable to function, but I insisted we go out to a taverna for a meal. I had a few sips of a beer, a few mouthfuls of food and promptly fell asleep at the table. I wasn't making any sense and Anne took me home to call the doctor and describe my symptoms.

The doctor told her to stop my Lithium dosage immediately and get my blood tested. The tests came back later that evening and they said that I was suffering from Lithium toxicity. Any more and I could have died or suffered internal organ failure, meaning dialysis for life. As I said, Lithium is incredibly effective, but also can be incredibly dangerous.

The very next week, Anne's father died.

Jack (*'Jicko'*) was a kind, gentle soul. I could chat to him all day and evening and often did. He was fascinating and lived one hell of a life. He grew up in Sunderland in the 1920s and 1930s. As Sunderland was a port, boats from all over the world brought cargo and often strange new diseases and child mortality was high.

When the Second World War broke out, he signed up to serve, first as a motorcycle despatch rider in Salisbury, then he transferred to serve in Burma. He always said he was one of the lucky ones, his war experiences were relatively tame compared with what many endured.

As a despatch rider, the standard issue motorbike was a Harley Davidson and he adored riding it, although he said that the back of the bike had a tendency to slip out around corners, so he and his colleagues used to weigh it down with bricks in the panniers.

His time in Burma started with a six week journey by boat to India. He was seasick throughout (a trait he has passed on to Anne, who can't even watch someone on a rowing boat on TV without feeling ill) and then of course there was always the constant fear of U-boat attacks. Their base was a stop off point for the front line and as such, many soldiers passed through. He got to meet former child actor and Charlie Chaplin co-star Jackie Coogan, who had signed up for the US Air Force during WWII and would later go on to play Uncle Fester in the US TV series The Addams Family. I won't repeat it here, but Jackie made a filthy and ungallant remark to Jack about his estranged wife, Betty Grable, and it became a tradition that if Jack told that story to a boyfriend of Anne or her sister, he was alright in Jack's eyes and you were accepted into the family! I was delighted when he eventually told me and felt that I had arrived. It was even funnier because Jack was notoriously prudish about swearing and anything deemed 'rude' so it was indeed an honour for him to trust me enough to tell all!

When the war started to turn, Jack's base was the first to receive the former prisoners of war from Changi Jail, Singapore, who had suffered horrifically under the Japanese occupation. I remember Jack telling me that they had advance warning of the POWs coming and everyone donated some of their rations to feed them, such as tinned Canadian bacon ('gorgeous' apparently), bread and tea. They had a tea urn and were ready to serve bacon sandwiches to their new guests. These were wolfed down and then almost immediately thrown up. The poor people had been treated so badly, fed almost nothing and their digestive systems just couldn't handle the rich food.

Jack emerged relatively unscathed, although he did contract malaria, something that would recur throughout his life. His only 'war wound' was when he tripped over a tent peg and cut his leg.

I remember fondly sitting there drinking whisky while he told me story after story of that era. When word finally came through that the Japanese had surrendered, he realised that he had never fired his pistol in the entire war, so asked permission from his superiors to let a few rounds loose.

The Army then had to decide how to repatriate such a large number of people. They decided on a classification system, based upon your skills. The UK had been devastated and needed rebuilding and so people with the appropriate experience would be sent back first. Jack told me how he could have kicked himself when he honestly replied that before the war he was a brick maker, as he hated the job and if he'd just kept quiet he could have had another 6-12 months out in the sun, rather than being immediately shipped back as Category A.

Later in life he became a rent collector on some of Sunderland's toughest estates and worked his way up to Area Housing Manager. One day, aged 62, he suffered chest pains and was taken to hospital. The doctors performed all the requisite tests and said there was nothing wrong with his heart, suggesting that it was stress related. He did have a horribly stressful job after all.

That weekend he looked into when he could retire on a full pension and by absolute chance he discovered it was that following Monday, so he retired that very day.

He announced to his family that he just wanted 'to sit on the sofa, watch football, drink whisky and smoke cigarettes' and, God bless him, he did *exactly* that for just a few months short of thirty years. He died just 2 months short of his 91st birthday.

We immediately flew back to be with Anne's Mum, her sister and to help arrange the funeral and deal with the countless other bits of paperwork associated with a loved one passing away. Now *I* had to be the strong one for Anne.

OK, 2016 must surely be over now? Surely?

Not so fast …

2016 had one final sting in its tail. I woke early one November morning to find that the United States, in their wisdom, and with their complicated electoral system, had elected a racist, sexist, four times bankrupt, orange, reality TV buffoon as President for the next four years.

Seriously!? I was fresh out of a psychiatric ward and even *I* could see this was not a good idea!

I remember thinking that no year had ever trolled me like they did in 2016, however I wrote this Chapter in July 2020 …

Chapter Nineteen: Things I have learned In Greece, Another Occasional List

After such a horrible chapter, I think something a bit lighter is in order. This is a list of things I have learned about living in Greece and the Greek people over the past decade, as usual, in no particular order whatsoever.

1. There Is Nothing Better Than a Day Spent at a Deserted Beach With a Cool Bag Full of Beers, Throwing Sticks for the Dog into the Sea.

The cooling off part isn't all bad either.

Anne and Floyd, Delfinia Beach, Stoupa

2. It Costs More to Feed and Vaccinate All Our Cats Than It Does To Pay My Mortgage in London.

My estimate is that each cat costs us about €1,000 a year, even when we import their food from Germany, which, including postage, is half the local prices. This figure doesn't include vet bills and it also doesn't include feeding the strays as well. We always have cheaper tins of food in the boot and in our rucksack for the strays, plus I have a family of 'bin cats' at the end of my road to feed each day.

3. Turn Your Modem Off When There is (Greece) Lightning

The last modem that blew was from the first lightning strike in a storm that was a direct hit on the house. We had no chance to turn everything off. There is nothing you can do to fix them at that point in time. Once the rain has passed you are generally OK.

4. Air Conditioning is a Must

I do know people that live without air conditioning, but not many. It is most definitely needed for at least three months of the year when the evening temperatures often don't drop below 28 degrees; a fan just won't cut it.

5. ... As is Some Kind of Winter Heating

Though the winters are generally mild compared with the UK, you definitely need some kind of heating. Many houses such as ours have central heating using heating oil. We have an open fire and two wood burners for evenings or extremely wet and cold days. Electric heaters use stupid amounts of energy and are incredibly costly.

6. Every Now and Again, Mother Nature Reminds You Who Is Boss

September 7th 2016 is the best example of this, but there hasn't been a year ago by without incredibly strong winds. I once saw my PVC greenhouse fly past a window. We've seen twisters out in the sea in front of our house and rains worse than any monsoon I have experienced in South East Asia. Oh yes - and earthquakes. We have only experienced two so far, but the house certainly moved.   In September 1986 an earthquake measuring 6.2 on the Richter scale hit Kalamata, although it was also felt around here too. Estimates vary, but between 23-35 people died and approximately 75% of the city was destroyed.

7. Many People in Greece Don't Like Laws

One of the things I love about the Greeks is that they like a nice relaxing life and laws just sometimes get in the way of things. London life - in particular relating to traffic wardens - was getting a bit rigid and moving here was just the tonic. For a start, in ten years I have only seen one single traffic warden.

Greeks are also very good at getting around whatever law is put into place. When we first came out here we noticed lots of people on motorbikes with their helmets not on their heads, but instead hanging from their wrist. A Greek friend explained to me just how and why this occurs.

In the UK we have Statute and Case Law or precedent. The Statute is the law that is passed by Parliament, written down. Case Law then evolves as and when new situations arise, where the Judge rules that Statute should be interpreted in a certain way. This means that there is now a precedent and so the law is evolving; ever changing.

In Greece you only have Statute, no Case Law or precedent, so the law is exactly how it is written down, with no modifications. When the law was passed that compelled Greek citizens to wear helmets when riding motorbikes, some imaginative legal brain took a look at the exact wording of the law and realised that the law didn't state explicitly *where* the helmet had to be worn, hence hanging a helmet off the wrist complied with the letter of the law, if perhaps not the spirit in which it was intended.

We sometimes get traffic police from Kalamata in our area, but it is rare. I am told that they are instructed to either catch people breaking the speed limit or not wearing seatbelts, however they implement only one of those instructions at any one time, not both.

So, for example, on a day when they are instructed to catch speeding motorists, if you drive by under the limit, but not wearing a seatbelt, you will not be stopped.

On another day when they are instructed to catch people not wearing seatbelts, you could drive past well over the limit, but if you are wearing a seatbelt you will be OK.

On top of that, most new cars have an alert that sounds when you drive above a certain limit without a seatbelt. Shops here sell 'fake' seatbelts, so only the metal part fits into the buckle, so that you can use it to 'trick' the car operating system into thinking you are actually wearing a seatbelt. Only in Greece.

Lastly, the Greek love of smoking is another legal challenge. They have introduced the smoking ban three times now for enclosed spaces and each time it has been largely ignored.

Of course, there are also huge negatives to this world view and some argue that while the UK has gone too far one way, Greece has gone way too far the other way - tax evasion for example.

8. 'Beggars *Can* Be Choosers'

We have adopted a fair few stray cats. A couple of those were being looked after at the Pantazi beach shelter, but the majority were just street cats, getting by any way that they could. Many would beg for food in the tavernas in the bay, while others would stay by the bins and dip in to get whatever they could from the refuse.

Either way, they were eating sporadically and badly. Whenever we take a cat in we always feed them the cheapest cat food that we can get to keep costs down. But within two months they will all turn their noses up at all but the most premium of cat sachets - not tins thank you very much! - and expect tuna or Alaskan line caught pollock heated up for them.

9. A Gas Camping Stove is a Very Wise Investment

We bought our gas camping stove in 2010 when austerity was being debated in the Greek Parliament and there were quite a few power cuts in protest. It has been a Godsend ever since. In general, the power supply here is good, especially in the summer. During winter, however, there are often planned outages for maintenance work etc, done when the tourists are not here. We are given advance warning on a website and so they are normally pretty easy to deal with. However, during heavy storms the power supply is intermittent and there have also been incidents with cars hitting electricity pylons etc.

We have cooked at least 15 evening meals during our time here on the stove, by candle light and with Anne holding a torch.

10. Smile Your Way Through Bureaucracy

You will experience bureaucracy, it is inevitable and much of it is maddening. It will sometimes take a few trips to get one simple job done and there will be many occasions where you just cannot see any logical reason to do what you are being asked to do. But the single worst thing that you can do is to lose your temper - it will take you twice as long, if not more.

11. Strimming Fields is The Devil's Work

I turn my hand to almost anything that won't get us killed - electrics, plumbing etc - but as I mentioned earlier, I have sworn to never, ever strim ever again. You start out fine for a minute. Broken cord. Replace. Five minutes later, start again - broken cord. For every minute of strimming there was maybe five to ten of maintenance.

Nope - pay someone. Crack a beer and listen to someone else take the strain. Then once it is all over, pay the man, crack another beer and enjoy one of the best sights in Greece - a freshly strimmed olive grove … done by someone else.

12. Nothing Tastes As Good As Your 'Home Grown' Fruit, Vegetables and Eggs.

Tomatoes fresh off the vine, peaches straight from the tree, oranges picked to juice for breakfast, letting the chickens out in the morning and coming back with a few fresh eggs to cook up. The food hasn't sat in a supermarket for days, you know exactly how it has been grown and it is the product of your own hard work over many months.

You will not, or cannot, ever go back. Even the so-called 'free range' eggs from the supermarket have nothing near the taste of our own, with their burnt orange coloured yolks.

13. The Garden Perimeter Wall is Always The First Thing Built on a Construction Project

I've seen so many construction projects over the years. In my mind I would build the house then at the end, build the wall around the garden - but not the Greeks. They almost always start building the perimeter wall first. I just don't get this. Why? I've even asked builder friends, received an answer, but I am still none the wiser. If you know the answer, please get in touch.

14. Greece Never Fails to Surprise You

Despite living in our present location for eight years, it was only in 2019 that we heard about a huge amphitheatre just a few miles away, past the mountain village of Platsa. It is so close to us that we can even see our house from it. We drove there one Spring day with Floyd to explore and it was truly stunning - what a venue!

Swervedriver's most iconic show to date - Platsa, autumn 2019. The peninsula behind me is Agios Nikolaos and behind the last bank of seats is our house.

The audience is seated facing the Mediterranean and cool winds blow through the surrounding pine trees. Only upon speaking to some locals did we realise that it wasn't really a venue at all. Indeed, the whole story was very Greek. It was built at great expense, by whom I don't know, and the first event was a play. That evening, they realised that they had forgotten to build any toilets for the audience and the local Dimos shut it down. It has remained closed ever since. All that work for one single event!

I took a live recording of my favourite band plus some battery powered iPad speakers and played it loud there, meaning that my beloved Swervedriver were, to the best of my knowledge, the first and only band to ever play this wonderful venue.

15. Never Buy Pre-packed Feta in the Supermarket

In the delicatessen counters there are large stainless steel tanks that contain the best tasting Feta you will ever eat and it is half the price of the packet stuff. And twice as tasty. Kalavrita is my favourite, which has an extra 'goaty' taste - believe me, this is a good thing.

16. Always Cuddle Your Animals Whenever You Pass Them

This is a rule of mine and it can sometimes prove problematic and time consuming, but it is rewarding. You never know what will happen tomorrow and so I always give a stroke, a pet or a cuddle to any animal I pass. Without wanting to sound corny, it could be your last.

It does, however, cause a few problems. I will go downstairs sometimes, see Floyd, Frankie, any of the others and have a great cuddle. Then I'll come back upstairs having completely forgotten to do the task I wanted to achieve.

Me, The Renegade Franklin and Floyd, early 2020.

This is the last time I ever cuddled Franklin - my favourite cat. She went off on one of her missions as she always did … but never came back. It's tough to know what to do. Cats go on walkabouts, but where do you start to look in thousands of acres, with snakes, foxes and jackals? RIP, The Renegade Franklin - you were just perfect and I miss you every single day. This place just isn't the same without you.

Chapter Twenty: 2017, Athens, Acropolis Now!

I have very little memory of 2017. My doctor told me that the brain can erase memories as a way of self-preservation, but that doesn't explain how I can remember lots about being in a psychiatric ward, the true low point of my life. Memory loss is also one of the many side effects of Lithium, but I started taking it a year previously. All in all, the year was something of a write-off.

I didn't work for the first half of the year, with Anne once again taking the strain for us both. The one issue that dominated the year was Anne's Mam, Jean. She was already suffering the early stages of dementia, but after Anne's dad Jack died, her decline was rapid; it was more of a spiral from the very day he passed away.

She was living in sheltered housing, with staff on hand to help if she called them, but she rarely, if ever, pulled the cord for help. We organised for a carer to come in four times a day to help her get washed and dressed, have breakfast, lunch and dinner and be put to bed, but it really wasn't enough. She regularly fell and was admitted to hospital a few times. We felt helpless being so far away and unable to be there for her the whole time. Anne's sister, Dot, lives in Glasgow - four hours' drive away - and she drove down regularly, which made us feel guilty as well as helpless. It was a huge undertaking and Dot was doing way more than her fair share.

We held crisis talks and agreed that we should suggest to Jean that she should go into a home with full time care. I know quite a few people whose parents have refused point blank to go into a home, but it really wasn't a problem here. I think the dementia meant that Jean didn't really know what was going on.

It is horrible watching someone you love deteriorate and it is sadly likely that many of you will experience this, or similar, to cherished family members. Jean showed classic signs of dementia, starting off with her being uncharacteristically snappy to both Anne and Dot, and also to Jack when he was alive. Then there was the forgetfulness and the general lack of understanding about what is going on around you. She didn't mean it, it is just a horrible, cruel disease.

Once the decision was made, we started a thoroughly draining seven month battle with Social Services. Care homes cost more than five star hotels, Jean had no savings and Social Services in the UK are strapped for cash. Who should pay? I always thought that we would receive 'cradle to the grave' care, but it was explained to me that this means hospital treatment and not care homes.

The Social Services people were brilliant and I have the utmost respect for them. They were honest and upfront, explained that they completely agreed with our case, but that the rules meant Jean wouldn't get full cover for the cost. They did all that they could, but were ultimately hamstrung by the rules and the scarcity of funding. We went through a rigorous assessment - Jean had dementia, she couldn't walk, she couldn't dress herself or put herself to bed, she couldn't prepare meals, she could barely hear or see - you would think that she was deserving of help, but you would be wrong.

While Jean was in hospital following a fall, someone broke into her flat in the sheltered housing complex and stole a load of her possessions, including wedding rings, other jewellery etc. The only upside - and I am really struggling to be positive here - was that we spoke with Social Services to explain the situation and it is possible that this sorry event speeded up the process and she was given approval to move to a home with full time care.

Jean's dementia meant that she just didn't realise what had happened and we didn't tell her. We were heartbroken though. There really wasn't much of monetary value taken, but the sentimental value was immense and the thought of people inside Jean's flat was horrifying. Seriously - what kind of lowlife breaks into a sheltered housing complex?

We then had to agree with Social Services how the home would be paid for. In the end, we were told that out of Jean's fairly generous monthly private and state pension, she would receive a whole £5 a week for treats, toiletries etc and the remainder would go to Social Services, who would cover the rest of her care. Getting old is thoroughly degrading - these are the people that gave birth to us and raised us.

We researched homes and arranged viewings while Dot drove down to visit them. We all agreed on a fantastic place on the outskirts of Sunderland and made arrangements to move her in.

It is never a simple task to travel to the UK. We have to leave Floyd with my friend Eirini, where she runs around with her best friend, a boxer called Romilia, all day and comes back thoroughly shattered. Then we need to arrange for the cats to be fed twice a day. Our neighbour does this and looks after the chickens, while keeping all the vegetables and trees watered. We also have some friends who happily house/dog/cat/chicken sit for us when they can.

The tasks were to box all Jean's stuff up, take certain items to the charity shop, move what possessions she wanted and needed to the care home, get the current flat redecorated and cleared/cleaned, move Jean in to her new home … and eat our body weights in Chinese, Indian, Thai and fish and chips! For some reason the Greeks aren't massive fans of spicy food. The nearest Chinese and Indian is an hour away. I would guess that as Greece has had net emigration rather than immigration that the joys of Asian cuisine haven't permeated as deeply into society as the UK.

Jean's move was successful and we returned to Greece. The past few years had been dominated by my poor health and the health of Anne's parents. We were constantly expecting calls that Jean had fallen again, but now we knew she was in a fantastic place with around the clock care. It seemed like a new start for us; indeed it was.

What better way to finally relax than to go on holiday? I remember being a kid at airports and they were just so exciting. It was a flurry of activity, eating McDonalds, all with the joy of knowing you would go somewhere different and probably warm. Now in my late 40s, that excitement has long faded. I hate airports, rules and regulations, always getting stopped by customs, planes, and, yes, if I am being honest . . . *people.*

No more planes for me unless I had to. This holiday was going to be by car and was going to be ... in Athens. We had lived in Greece for six years and other than going to the airport had never spent any time in the capital city. We did some research and decided to stay on the Athens Riviera, to the south of the city. Glyfada was a name that came up, it was on the coast and was the former playground of Jackie Onassis and other 1960s icons. It was also on the tram line into central Athens, so it sounded perfect.

Who am I kidding? If I am truly honest, we found out that there was a Marks & Spencer shop there and we wanted to fill the car up at the end of our break with tubs of cornflake cakes, steak bakes, pies, curries, fruit sherbets etc.

Within a few hours of arriving we were kicking ourselves that we hadn't been here before properly. Glyfada was stunning, a bit like Highgate-on-Sea, full of swish shops and restaurants. If you did a survey on which is the best European city within 3.5 hours' flight from London, I'd bet Athens wouldn't make the top 10 or even 20. It should. It should be in the top 5. Yes, I adore Paris, Amsterdam, Rome, Barcelona etc, but really, Athens has it all - history, sun, beaches, shopping, food. You can get 5 star hotel rooms for €150, including breakfast for two, eaten on a terrace overlooking the Acropolis.

We took the tram into the centre of Athens, Syntagma Square, the location of the Greek Parliament and the scene of rioting in years gone by. Just down from that is Plaka, two main streets that run parallel to each other with amazing shops. Plaka reminded me of Camden Market, with a great flea market at the end.

Towering above all this is the Acropolis, which is simply breathtaking. I'd been doing some reading beforehand about it and discovered the story of a Greek hero who recently passed away, called Manolis Glezos. Under Nazi occupation in May 1941, the Greek flag at the Acropolis had been taken down and replaced with the Swastika. Under the cover of darkness, Manolis and a friend sneaked into the Acropolis past Nazi guards and replaced it with the Greek flag. It inspired the resistance and the perpetrators were sentenced to death in absentia, but were not caught until much later.

But the story of Manolis Glezos doesn't end there. I grew up watching World War II movies and still love them now. In the films, the British and the Greek were always on the same side, fighting a common enemy. Indeed, historically, the British and the Greeks have been natural allies with common foe. The British helped overthrow the Turkish rule of Greece in 1821, a revolution that started in Areopoli, just 45 minutes' drive south of our house here. But it wasn't until I moved here that I started to learn about the dark past of the British at the end of the war.

Greece suffered horribly in World War II. Proportionately, Greece had more deaths than almost any other country in the war, with only Lithuania and Poland recording more. Of course on an absolute basis, the Soviet Union lost an estimated 20 million people. There was widespread hunger and with limited supplies of food, Churchill was forced to make a decision as to whether Bengal (also experiencing a famine, but part of the British Empire) or Greece should receive food aid. He chose Bengal. When the organisation Oxfam is mentioned, people often think of more recent famines in Ethiopia, but its first campaign was actually in Greece in 1943.

Towards the end of World War II, Churchill was increasingly worried about the spread of Communism and saw Greece as a likely candidate to fall under Soviet influence, giving them a base on the Mediterranean. In 1944, British soldiers, with the bizarre assistance of former Nazi soldiers/mercenaries, machine gunned a crowd of innocent civilians in Syntagma Square. Later, fighter planes strafed supposed 'left wing' neighbourhoods in Athens.

As revenge, Manolis Glezos, with the assistance of 30 other Greek resistance fighters, decided to blow up the British HQ, situated in The Hotel Grande Bretagne. To do this, he crept through miles of sewers on Christmas Day 1944, placing a ton of dynamite under the target. He came out of the sewer stinking, was washed down and waited for the order to detonate. It never came. Winston Churchill had made an unexpected visit to Athens and was in the building. The resistance didn't want to kill one of 'The Big Three' (Churchill, Roosevelt, Stalin) and so the plan was aborted.

Churchill later sent a telegram to his wife: "You will have read about the plot to blow up HQ The Hotel Grande Bretagne. I do not think it was for my benefit. Still, a ton of dynamite was put in sewers by extremely skilled hands."

Those extremely skilled hands belonged to Manolis Glezos, who later became the oldest serving MEP, at 92.

After a particularly long and liquid Thai lunch near Plaka we both decided to get tattoos. It was my one concession to a midlife crisis. After all, I couldn't buy a Harley Davidson as the roads and drivers are too dangerous and a leather jacket would be too hot in Greek weather.

I got lyrics from my favourite Swervedriver song on my right forearm and Anne got my name tattooed on her ring finger. It didn't hurt that much, but then I had stashed a bottle of Jack Daniels in the toilet. The poor guy must have worried about my bladder as I made several 'visits' during the 90 minute session.

Our final hours in Athens were spent basically swiping whole shelves into the trolley at Marks & Spencer. We left there about €400 lighter.

Back at home, my mania was running at high levels. Lithium is a great stabiliser, but it doesn't fully stop me going in either direction. If 0 is complete depression, needing a Zyprexa to knock me out and reset my brain and 10 is full-on mania - both levels I used to reach - I would now alternate between a 3 and 8. I was at eight. The thing about mania is that it is really fun. In fact, I really used to miss it when I started my medication. Once on the Lithium, life just seemed … *flat*. With full-on mania you feel invincible, you constantly come up with new ideas, plans. Often I would wake up to find whole lists of things that I just *had* to do. 90% of them are garbage, but the 10% are often rather inspired. I filter them out, hide them from Anne when I can, although she often finds them first. One idea I came up with stood up to scrutiny in the cold light of day. I begged Anne to allow me to start the project and she probably decided to let me do it just to shut me up.

That is how we ended up having a cat walkway in our living room, high up off the ground, a series of linked shelves where the cats can sleep knowing that they cannot be attacked by anyone or anything. It took a fair bit of prodding and cajoling, but after a week they loved it and often queue up to use it.

The year ended with us collecting driftwood down at Pantazi Beach after a particularly bad storm. It's always best to go there after a storm as the waves bring in the best free fuel for our wood burner, together with the usual rubbish, which almost always includes a sole flip flop. I often wonder: Who? How? Why? When?

As we were loading the car up we saw our friends Chris and Sue, who feed the stray cats down at Pantazi. We stopped for a chat and Chris was somewhat upset. A group of kittens that were born in the storeroom of one of the Stoupa shops had been dumped there. He had found out who it was through the grapevine and demanded that they take the kittens back, which they did, although one had escaped and couldn't be caught at the time. Chris showed him to us and we fell in love. He was a cappuccino tabby, so a regular tabby cat, but with a face and breast of light brown, plus a spotty belly like a leopard. There were numerous cats with similar markings in the village and for some reason they all seemed to be incredibly friendly. This young man was no exception. He sat on my lap and just purred. In fact, I have a photo of the exact moment. I posted it on Facebook that very day.

We just *KNEW* ...

I think you can probably guess where this is going.

We took him home, cleaned his ears of mites and fed him his first meal on our bed, where he stayed for about two weeks.

As usual, we had him vaccinated and checked out by our friendly vet. We have never had any adverse reactions, but unfortunately with this poor chap we did. We stayed up all night with him, fearing he would die as he seemed so weak. Luckily after 24 hours he regained some strength and we relaxed.

Now we needed a name. After a bit of thought we settled on the name Oswald, or Ozzy for short, keeping the musical name tradition alive. I'd loved Ozzy Osbourne as a kid, in fact I still love him now and his guitar player Randy Rhoads was an inspiration for me when I was learning, however I'm not quite sure that Randy is a good name for a cat; I can't imagine shouting that from the front door.

One day in 1982, on tour, Ozzy's band were offered a chance to fly in a small plane. Randy went in the plane, but Ozzy stayed in the tour bus, sleeping off a hangover. The pilot decided to 'buzz' the bus to wake Ozzy up, but the wing of the plane clipped the bus and they crashed, killing everyone in the plane. Randy was just 25. Ozzy is only alive because he had spent the previous night getting wasted. Musicians and planes are a horrible combination.

Within hours we knew that young Oswald was an absolute stunner. Perhaps because he was taken from his mother at such a young age he saw us as surrogate parents, but he would lie on my stomach when I am in bed and nuzzle my neck. He still does it to this day, it is as part of the morning routine as tea and biscuits.

Cat number TEN! Double figures!

(A good friend of ours who house sits here when we go back to the UK said to me later that as soon as she saw the photo of me meeting the kitten that would become 'Ozzy' that she KNEW we would adopt him. Perhaps it is a safe bet, but it did make me laugh).

Cheeky from the beginning, Ozzy on the floor, harassing Huck.

Chapter Twenty One: 2018, Greek Mosaics

After the upheaval of the previous years and the relative calm in the second half of last year we both said that we would be happy with a nice, average year, with no drama and we pretty much achieved that. It was a nice mixture of paid work, work on the house and garden, free time, lounging about, swimming and generally relaxing.

For the first time since we arrived, I actually had some free time to devote to a hobby. As I previously mentioned, one of my friends asked me when I told him about our move 'won't you get bored out there?' Bored? I haven't had the time to be bored! We wake at six and although we go to bed very early, we are literally on our feet and active every minute, bar 20 minutes for each meal.

For quite a while I had wanted to do a mosaic course and I saw a flyer promoting a one day introductory course in a nice shady courtyard in the neighbouring village of Kardamyli. The course was run by an incredibly friendly and knowledgeable Canadian/Greek lady and I adored it. I left with a half decent recreation of the Primal Scream 'Screamadelica' album cover and a brand new passion for mosaics.

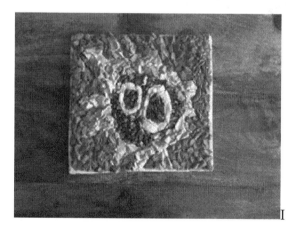

'Don't fight it, feel it'.

Instantly I wanted to start my second project and had been promising Anne that I would paint us a house sign, but now it felt that a mosaic was more fitting. There are very few addresses in our area, our road doesn't even have a name and we get our post delivered to the supermarket, so a house name would give us at least some identity. We had decided to call the house 'Rizes' meaning 'new roots' or just 'roots' in Greek. The expression '*kalo riziko*' is said to people who buy a new house - 'happy new roots, new life' and rice, '*rizi*', is thrown at newlyweds instead of confetti here for similar reasons.

The first mosaic was the size of a seven inch single. The house sign was about twice that size. For my next project I went somewhat bigger; in fact, stupidly bigger.

We had a very ugly concreted area at the bottom of the field, about the size of 2.5 car parking spaces. I decided to mosaic the whole thing, estimating that it would take me about two months. It ended up taking me eleven months. Worse than that, I was so determined to do it that I started in August, with heat of over 40 degrees.

I'd sit out there under my parasol with just a pair of shorts on, with Floyd and Alan, my favourite hen, for company.

L-R: Floyd, Alan, Me, summer 2018

Time just flew. I'd go out at 9am, spend what seemed like half an hour cutting and laying tiles and then suddenly it would be lunch time. Siestas were out, I was too excited getting this done. I'd tile for what seemed like another half hour and then it would be 5pm! For years I had battled to keep mania at bay with meds, diet, exercise etc. Meditation was a no-no for me, I am too restless. Now by complete accident I had found the solution! Bipolar often means that your mind is flitting between many different subjects and it can be incredibly draining, but out there in the field with my trusty dog and my trusty hen, all that mattered was the next tile - cut properly, pasted down and then finally grouted then wiped down. Anne said that I would be in a trance like state for at least 30-45 minutes afterwards.

If the end product looks like it was made up by a madman as he went along, then that is probably not far from the reality. I had the main idea of a sun in the middle with swirling sections coming out from the centre like a whirlwind. Each of these sections was filled with items that were to be found in the area of the field that particular section pointed to, so for example the section leading to the polytunnel had pop art tomatoes in it. The section leading to the chickens had a rooster and some fried eggs. The orange and lemon trees had slices of each fruit, meaning I could get a reference to the debut Stone Roses record cover in under the radar. Other sections had a snake, the design of which I found when looking through my GSCE Art sketch books, a load of bees next to the water fountain and rosemary. You get the picture. I adored every single minute of it.

As to the finished product, I blow hot and cold really. I'm immensely proud of it, but I'm not sure I really like it as a whole. It looks like it was made with no plan (which it was) and it was a stupidly ambitious project to attempt when I was still learning the craft. I see mistakes everywhere. I used the wrong grout. I had limited colours for tiles, many of which I got for free by just asking if I could take any broken ones from a builders' yard. Why buy new ones just to break? Some days I toy with the idea of concreting over it and starting afresh.

Anyway, you be the judge:

One of my favourite comments was from a friend in Moscow who said 'I absolutely love the idea that in a thousand years' time, archaeologists will find that and go 'what … the … hell!?''

When we moved into the house there was a large plot of land to one side of us. It had been scrub land for about four decades and the owner wanted a ridiculous price for it, which was fine by us as it meant no one would buy it and develop it. But recently we had noticed that a local agent had been showing people around and there was a fair bit of interest.

One day we were doing 20 lengths of the pool with Floyd running around and herding us, when two heads popped up over the wall and both said hello. We replied in a not particularly friendly manner and asked if we could help them. 'Oh no, don't mind us, we're just having a look around. We're thinking of buying this land and building a house here'. Oh. No. You're. Not. Previously we had planned that whenever we saw prospective land purchasers we would put on some of Anne's most offensive punk records at full volume and I would walk past naked with Floyd on a lead and say hello, but we had been caught on the hop here.

Anne and I had a very brief chat and decided there was no way we wanted either a building site or neighbours; no way. New builds can take as long as two years and some just stop part way through, leaving an ugly concrete structure, sometimes for decades. They are incredibly noisy and messy and often build right through siesta and illegally on Sundays. We've had builds near us before and it is horrible. I should point out that we also had our own building project, when we had the pool installed, so there is more than a hint of hypocrisy in our viewpoint, although ours was a short project. We decided to go down and buy the land. The agent said that the vendor wouldn't take an offer - it was full price or no deal. We offered the full asking price and shook on it.

My experiences with housing transactions have been long and tortuous. There has never been an easy one, just shades of terrible. I tend to find that housing and people are a toxic combination and people regress 30 years to being unreasonable, spoiled children. I made it very clear to the agent that I am straight down the line, fair, honest and transparent. I regard a handshake as a deal and if I say I will do something, I will do it. She assured me that everything would be fine. A mere three hours later she called to say there had been a mistake in pricing the land and the owner now wanted 20% more.

Were the land just another plot we'd have walked away there and then. Life is too short to deal with energy-sapping flakes. But it wasn't any other plot. It was the one right next to us and we were forced buyers; buyers of a plot that we didn't even want. We relented and offered the full amount. Next came a tortuous five months where the legal situation of the land was assessed. I'll spare you a long boring essay on Greek property law, but just a few pertinent points:

1. The system isn't bad, it is not too dissimilar to the UK system, itself more than slightly flawed.

2. You need to check title and planning permission. You also need to check that the land isn't classed as Forestry land, as building is completely forbidden on such land. Any house built on Forestry land will be torn down, in fact I know of a few in the area that have suffered this fate. Imagine having to pay someone to tear down your own house. The Forestry certificate is the thing that takes the time.

3. Planning permission can take time and depends where your land is.

4. Agents charge the buyer 2% and the vendor 3%, taking fees from both sides of the deal. It is standard, but it is also one hell of a conflict of interest. How can they act in the best interests of both parties? A good deal for one is by definition a bad deal for the other, it is a zero sum game. It stinks.

5. Additional fees and taxes come to between around 11%-13% of the value of the land/house.

6. As ever, it is the people involved, not the system that makes it difficult, sometimes almost intolerable.

7. Laws change frequently, get a good lawyer.

    After months of legal work, our solicitor advised us that the vendor cannot prove sole title to the land, plus there was a doubt over whether planning permission would be granted. Despite all the trouble, this wasn't a bad outcome for us. It meant that we didn't have to buy it and also meant that no one else would buy it.

A few months later we received another call from our solicitor and she informed us that both issues had now been resolved and we would need to consider buying the land again.

Bored of property troubles yet? I know I am. Let's move on to something better. I hadn't spoken a word to my parents in several years. We both said some incredibly hurtful things and didn't see eye to eye on several subjects. We had been so close and they had been amazing, loving and supportive parents, bringing up what we now know to be a troubled son. I have no idea what prompted this, but one day I decided that this couldn't go on. We'd have to accept that we would never agree on certain things and not discuss them again, then attempt to rebuild what had previously been a fantastic relationship for 40 years. I called them out of the blue, we had a chat for over an hour and they promised to come out and see us shortly. It felt great.

I was cleaning out the chickens one hot July evening when Anne called me back urgently. Marley had let out a huge squeal and was lying down panting, obviously not in a good way. We'd feared this day ever since we took her to the heart specialist vet in Kalamata on our wedding anniversary in 2016. She'd had a heart attack and was slowly dying. We placed her on a comfy bed and just calmly stroked her as her life ebbed away, telling her how much we loved her. It took about 30 minutes and both Anne and I were in floods of tears. I've had so many animals and yet this was the first time anything like this had happened.

Back in 2016 the vet said she had maybe six months left in her, but she managed over two years. She came from a shelter in North London to Greece, had fields to hunt in, food on tap, she even had her own house, albeit a half-built empty one, down our road for a while. Even though I am getting upset typing this and reliving the experience, I am also extremely proud at the life we managed to give her.

I went out in the extreme heat and dug a grave, or to be precise, dug about six graves. The ground was so hard after months without rain and I kept hitting rock. We eventually found the right spot, placed her there, covered her up with earth, wood and rocks so no wild animals could get to her and said our last goodbyes. The next day I did my fourth mosaic, a large red M on slate for her grave. Sleep well my friend.

The last photo of Marley, two days before she died.

There are times in life when you feel cheated or feel that things are just not fair. Marley's death was horribly upsetting, particularly as we witnessed it, but she had enjoyed a great life. We didn't feel cheated; she had led a charmed existence for many years.

Around the same time, Sparky, the all black kitten with fierce green eyes we adopted from the seafront in Stoupa in 2012, went missing. Anne has a sixth sense about these things. She knows when the animals are sick and notices well before I do. It was not uncommon for Sparky to go missing on adventures for several days, sometimes up to a week.

A week had passed since we last saw and fed Sparks and Anne was getting worried. Knowing that she had a love of adventures and could go missing for long periods even in the heat of the summer, I was fairly relaxed, albeit with a hint of worry in the background.

We did the usual routine of putting up a 'Lost' post on local Facebook pages and animal groups, but I was fairly certain she would come home. We went on long walks all around the area early in the morning before the sun was at its height, shaking bags of her favourite treats, checking out known hideaways, but to no avail. We just had to sit and wait for her return.

A further week passed and now I was getting worried, Anne even more so. She sent emails to all of the surrounding neighbours, holiday villages and tavernas. I remember being out in the garden doing some work when Anne came out crying - one of the nearby holiday villas had replied to our email and said that they had found a dead cat matching Sparky's description the previous week. The timing and area was sadly correct, there were no other pure black cats within a 1km radius. It had to be her.

We were both in pieces - to lose a young (just six years old) lively, loving cat in circumstances unknown just wasn't fair, but then I remembered that my mother always said 'life just isn't fair'; a rather silly, throwaway comment, but sadly very true.

To this day we still don't know what happened to her. It was August, so there were far more cars down our road than usual, but then she wasn't found by the side of the road. She had no previous health issues and had been regularly vaccinated. To me, this just left an attack by a fox, jackal or snake, a car injury where she was able still to find cover … or poison. We will never know as we couldn't examine the body unfortunately.

To many, a house with eight cats in would seem full, or perhaps even excessive, but we felt their loss hugely. We had more love to give and one day a few weeks later, Anne mentioned a kitten that had caught her eye.

At the end of our road before the main road are the bins. Our part of Greece has communal bins that are emptied every few days, mostly, and they are often the place where stray cats hang out, mainly to eat from the bins, but also to try and ingratiate themselves with anyone stopping. Our lot don't do badly, not they would ever let on. Besides us, I know of at least three other people that feed them. They often have what I call 'bin nose', which is a filthy nose that is as a result of rifling through bags for scraps to eat.

Anne had seen a little calico kitten that had a problem with her eye. A calico is a cat that is white, black and orange and they are commonly found in Greece. This kitten always came up to Anne and was particularly friendly, purring and cuddling whenever Anne picked her up - their love was mutual.

Before adopting a cat it is necessary to find out more about it - how long it has been there, how it interacts with the rest of the group, how it got there. For example, there are stray cats that really have taken to the lifestyle, that have family there who would miss them. Many cats are best off left in the environment that they are thriving in, with their family and being fed by locals.

But it looked to us that this kitten might be losing the sight in one eye and we were worried it might lose its sight completely.

We decided to speak to a neighbour, Bill, a lovely chap who has fed and looked after the stray cats of our area for several years. He had been feeding this particular stray cat bin crew for years, so we asked him if it was OK to give this one a home. He gave us the nod, so we went to the bins and picked her up.

I watched the video that we took at the time just the other day and knowing what I know now, it was beautiful. She didn't have any objection whatsoever to Anne picking her up, and she came back with us in the car to become cat number nine in our house.

We immediately took her to the vet and he gave us a lotion to put in her good eye. I think it was €40, but what price sight?

Once again, she followed the tried and tested route of spending a few weeks in our bedroom with food served to her, just relaxing, she was neutered, chipped, vaccinated, then let out to live a new life; a life so different to her previous one, yet just 700m away.

The lotion saved her other eye. For all you cat owners out there, you know how difficult it is to just give a tablet to a reluctant cat. Try putting lotion on the eye of a former stray! I ended up wearing a hooded top in the midst of summer as I was scratched up so much, but perhaps a suit of armour would have been more fitting.

Now we had a wiry, short haired, one eyed calico, and we needed a name. At the time we were all out of musical names (although don't worry, we soon rediscovered our mojo quickly enough), so we decided on Ravioli ('Ravi').

Ravioli (Rav, Ravi, DJ Ravioli)

Ravi very quickly ruled the roost. She had the street cat in her, something that most of them had to differing degrees, but I'd never seen it like this. Any food that was put down 'communally' would be instantly hit upon by her, with growls to let the others know that she is in control and they better not bother trying to intervene. She is, without fail, the very first to be fed at breakfast time, a time that is often very stressful for us.

A small sub-set of the cats waiting for their breakfast

With Rav nicely settled in, we settled into autumn and the winter. One of our pastimes, which is a pastime with benefits, is to take Floyd walking along the beach and collect firewood for the wood burner in our bedroom. We went down there at the start of Halloween weekend. I threw sticks for Floyd into the sea, Anne started collecting wood.

After a while I came back to the car and noticed that a pretty pure black kitten, just like Sparky, had started winding its legs around Anne and generally being gorgeous. NO! Not another one, we have enough!

We filled an entire car load of firewood and there he still was. We'd seen him before in a local village and he was a long way from there. Perhaps he just wandered as cats do, perhaps he was dumped there? But what we did know was that he was right next to an establishment where the owner was notoriously violent to animals. And it was

Halloween, where black cats around the world are sadly discriminated against by some people, Greece being no different.

I think you can guess where this is going.

Back home to the usual routine.

We needed a name for him and he reminded us of another cat we had 'sort' of adopted back in London. To be fair he adopted us and, as it would turn out, at least a few other houses.

We had got home one day after work to find a huge black cat on our bed. At the time our cat flaps were not chip activated, so he had just walked in and made himself comfortable.

Other times we would find him asleep on my drum kit, but he caused no trouble with the others, so it didn't bother us. We found him one day with a huge cyst on his head and assumed that the owners would take care of it, but three days later there he was, asleep on the bed or the drum kit still with the huge cyst and we decided to get him seen by the vet, at a cost of £60.

A few days later we saw him with a pink diamanté collar on, like a pet owned by a James Bond villain, absolutely miserable. There followed notices from the owners on the lampposts to 'not feed this cat' (we never did) and it turned out he had been sleeping in at least two other houses apart from ours and his owners'.

We named that cat Marshall, as he slept on the drum kit next to the guitar amplifier of the same name and we thought that this was a good name for our new arrival, the newest member of our house.

Clockwise from Left: Marshall, Marshall, Marshall, Marshall.

Like me, any guitar geek will tell you how good Marshall amplifiers are. Look at any photo of any legendary lead guitar player (as opposed to bass) and you will see the iconic Marshall sign behind them. Hendrix used them (in fact his middle name is Marshall), Slash used them, John Frusciante of the Red Hot Chili Peppers used them; they are ubiquitous.

I also have a historical tie to Marshall amps. Back in the day, my Dad played bass in a band, 'The Hustlers', based in West London in the 1960s. He made his own amplifier, in fact hardly any good amps existed back then. He played a gig at a school, met a girl there and, well … do I need to say more? They have been together now for 60 years, I was born of rock n' roll, which might be one reason why I am so obsessed with it.

Dad's band used to get their instruments and hang out in their local music shop, when the owner invited them as the best band in the neighbourhood to come to the opening party for his new amplifier. The owner's name was Jim Marshall.

It's hard getting exact memories from those days, I would say more due to time than sex 'n drugs 'n rock 'n roll, but I do remember him telling me that Long John Baldry ('LJB') played at the opening party.

LJB gave Elton John his big break, as documented in the brilliant autobiography, 'Me'- although it should have been called 'I'm Still Standing' in my humble opinion - and also became a tenant of Rod Stewart when Rod's accountant said he was making too much money and needed to buy a new pad.

That house that Long John lived in was 50 yards away from our flat in Muswell Hill, where we first packed up a car to move to Greece. According to Rod Stewart, LJB had a pet goat and he would take it walking around Muswell Hill, including to the Post Office. Also living along our road were Amy Winehouse - she wrote 'Back to Black' there and moved to Camden when the royalties came in - and Carl Barât from The Libertines.

Just like the previous Marshall, our Marshall has decided that one home isn't good enough and he now spends most of his time at our neighbour's house, plus two other houses down our road.

Chapter Twenty Two: 2019, 'Boys in the Feta Land'

The land purchase rolled on and on. I'll save you the boredom, but we did finally - just - get it done in July 2019. It was perhaps the toughest property transaction I have ever completed in my life and it was simply for a piece of land, not even a house.

We didn't even want the land, we just didn't want anyone noisily building next to us for two years, or for it to become an Airbnb.

Greece often gets a bad rap for tax evasion and property law. I think the property law reputation has its merits, but it is mostly no worse than the English system. As with the English system, the major difficulty is just *people* being unreasonable.

The tax area is complicated. Where Greece is way more advanced than the UK is that everything is joined up, so if you want to sell a house or some land and you have outstanding income tax or even parking fines, you are stopped from completing the transaction. This is the situation we found ourselves in.

Our vendor had outstanding income tax that he had no money to pay - he wanted us to pay it so he could get the certificate of being tax free so he could then sell us the land. We were not happy obviously, but our great solicitor kept us calm and we did it, just to get the deal done.

Then we went to the Notary to complete things. Each point on the plot of land is mapped by GPS and then is read out by the Notary and agreed by the Solicitor. On a standard, square, UK garden that is 4 points, but on an old Greek terraced garden it was 24 points, each with two co-ordinates, X and Y, each of these with up to nine numbers including to the right of the decimal point.

Just as we were getting to the end, with the vendor's tax weighty bill paid, there was a power cut. Luckily, the final sheet still printed and we were done. Thirty seconds later and we would have come back another day, with no land and having paid a stranger's tax bill.

We now owned a new piece of Greece!

For five years now we had been struggling along with our two small chicken coops, the original Mr Blobby and the flat pack one. Our neighbour who went halves on chicken duties and eggs suggested that as we had the space we should build a walk in coop, which made cleaning far easier. She luckily had a friend who had built one already and was willing to help. This was great for many reasons, the first being that my DIY skills are 'average' to say the least. Perhaps 'average' is being charitable.

I remember in Craft, Design & Technology at school, my teacher once wrote tactfully in my report something like 'what Guy lacks in skill he makes up with in effort'.

Tony was a great guy, once a part of the touring crew with Hawkwind, featuring musical hero Lemmy, who himself was previously a roadie for Jimi Hendrix and would later form Mötörhead. We spent much of May chatting about music in between sawing and hammering.

It was around this time that I felt some sympathy with builders, as our original estimate was €600 and about three days of work. Due to a number of factors out of our control it cost nearer €1,200 and took three weeks, but I loved every minute of it.

We started by getting a concrete base laid with a brick surround, then built the structure, lining the inside with plywood and the outside with tongue and groove, weather proofing as we went along. The roof was steel, roof tile effect. Lastly, there were steps up to it which our neighbour plaka'd (crazy paving, essentially).

I thought it needed a bit of artwork, so knocked out a chicken mosaic in a day. Finally, such a fine structure needed a name, so I thought '*Cluckingham Palace*' would do the job.

Cluckingham Palace

It was a real labour of love, but the end result was definitely worth it. At its highest it was a little under 2.5m, with windows and vents on each side to keep a nice cool breeze going through. To the right as you entered were five nesting boxes and to the left were three bars of varying height for the hens to roost. They loved it immediately and Tony's design meant it stayed cool even at the height of summer.

Spoil our animals? Us?

In the next chapter I will be looking at the things that I miss about the UK and the things I don't miss. But in advance of that, the one thing I miss most is live music. A few bands play down in the village from time to time, but it is almost always way past my bed time.

Whenever a band I liked toured Europe, I would scour the listings for an Athens date, but hardly anyone came. A friend in the music business explained that for a promoter to put on a show they need to pay the act a large up front amount and then hope that firstly enough people buy tickets and hope that the currency stays stable. For our time in Greece to date there was enough uncertainty to mean that few people were willing to risk this.

Then we saw that a festival called 'Release' was on in Athens and had been running for some years, with the same stage used over approximately a month for a wide range of bands and DJs. Headlining one day were New Order, supported by Johnny Marr (formerly of The Smiths), Morcheeba and Fontaines DC.

The last time I had seen New Order was a quarter of a century ago, in my then home town of Reading, at the annual August Bank Holiday Festival. They played to approximately 50,000 people then; Release was just 5,000, perhaps fewer.

Johnny Marr has been a hero of mine for over 30 years, perhaps the only guitar hero of mine that I hadn't seen play live. I'd seen Morcheeba a few times and really liked them. As I had spent the last ten years in the middle of nowhere with no radio or friends to tell me what was good, I had never heard of Fontaines DC.

This was too good to miss, so we bought tickets. Tickets for the show were €40, which is a bargain, but you could also buy VIP tickets at €100 (which included free drinks), so we naturally went for the latter choice.

The venue was right by the sea, a few tram stops away from Glyfada, our usual place to stay in Athens.

My usual music venues were in London and you could be fairly sure that any band playing the numerous festivals in the UK would play a warm up show there, or if any band was touring they would play, so I was always out watching music. Within just five miles of our house we had The Kentish Town Forum, Dingwalls, Camden Electric Ballroom and the Jazz Café, where I once watched a band play a residency there five nights running.

Growing up in Reading, I went to the Festival every year for a decade, starting off with the year I got my GCSE results. I got my results then set up my tent! I was used to bad weather, rain and mud. Release was something else though - 35 degree heat, not a drop of rain, no mud, right next to the Mediterranean - perfect.

We arrived just as Fontaines DC came on to a tiny crowd of maybe 100 - 5 'youngsters' from my family ancestral home of County Mayo, Ireland. I'd checked out a few of their videos on YouTube and hadn't really been that keen on them to be honest, but it was just lovely to be watching live music again after nine long years. Either sound systems had improved massively over that time, or this one was particularly good, but they sounded *amazing*.

I've been lucky enough in my time to see a number of support bands or a band low on the bill of a festival who were destined for big things and who blew me away. Once, I was waiting to see a band from my school play at Reading Festival and got there early; just early enough to catch the end of the set of some kids from Seattle called Nirvana. Kurt ended the last song my diving into the drum kit, dislocating his shoulder in the process, a scene they include in the video for 'You Know You're Right'.

Fontaines DC were now added to that list. They'd only released their debut album, 'Dogrel', a few months previously and were part way through a punishing European tour, playing Glastonbury twice the next month. I loved them and think that album is perhaps the best record released in the last 20 years, better even than the two new albums by Swervedriver - praise indeed.

Fontaines DC playing Athens, Greece, 2019; 'The Boys in the Feta Land'

Morcheeba's set was great too, watched while Anne went and got beer after beer, as the sun went down over yachts moored in the adjacent marina.

But it was really Johnny Marr who I had come to see. I was initially a bit wary as he sings and plays guitar now, but having checked out some of his videos on YouTube I knew he would be good. However, I didn't know he'd be 'in the top 5 shows I have seen of all time' good. He started with 'Tracers' off his latest solo album, then straight into 'Bigmouth Strikes Again'. His band was absolutely amazing, as opposed to Morrissey's band who I saw in front of 200 people at the BBC before I left the UK and who were a little lame and lacklustre.

'How Soon is Now?' was epic, he included 'Stop Me if You've Heard This One Before', loads of great solo stuff, finishing off with 'There is a Light That Never Goes Out'. It really was perfection. Did I mention that Bernard Sumner from New Order came on for two Electronic songs too? 'This is my mate Barney from Salford' was the simple introduction.

I'm aware that writing this as a sad 46 year old I sound like a dad desperately trying to be cool, but I can assure you that, whilst sounding sad, it is truly from the heart. I live for music; I live for days like this.

How to follow that? New Order tried, but just didn't match it. For years now the animosity between Peter 'Hooky' Hook and the other three had been simmering, with both Barney and Hooky writing autobiographies and not being particularly complimentary about each other.

There are people that say that New Order without Hooky are not worth watching, and perhaps it was the fact that we'd spent a day in the sun, perhaps it was because it was past my bed time, but they just didn't do it for me. I sat watching them, eating burgers and drinking beers while Anne was off dancing at the front of the stage, as they were more her kind of thing.

It is a shameful admission that I had now spent nine years in Greece and never done an olive harvest. I had tried a few times before, but it just never worked out, for one reason or another. This year was the year, and I offered my services for free to my friend Eirini and family.

I had met Eirini several years previously as I needed a dog sitter for Floyd when we went back to the UK. She quickly became my best friend out here and her house became Floyd's second home.

Her two dogs are the only dogs that Floyd has any time for and we would walk them up the mountain that Eirini lived on and down to the beaches during the off-season.

Eirini spoke perfect English and was also a Greek teacher, so I resumed my lessons in an effort to crack the language. Her mother loved fresh eggs, so I would pay for my lessons with the produce of our hens.

These walks continue to this day and we hike for a little over two hours and speak only Greek the entire time. For every step we took, Floyd would take ten, wrestling and play fighting with her friends. Then afterwards we would have a coffee and go over my written homework, while she set me something for the next week.

It wasn't just the Greek language that Eirini would teach me, she also has an amazing knowledge of local plants and trees.

Back when I was younger I had two favourite TV shows, besides the usual A-Team and Dukes of Hazzard - Keith Floyd and Bush Tucker Man. I've already gone into some length about Keith Floyd, but Bush Tucker Man was unique.

Bush Tucker Man was also known as Major Les Hiddins of the Australian Army and wore a distinctive Abukra hat. The Australian Army wanted their soldiers to be able to live in the Australian bush and rain forests, to be able to survive off the land should there be an invasion and Major Les Hiddins was given the task of gathering the knowledge, mainly from indigenous Aboriginal tribes.

He made a TV series about it and it fascinated me. They are all on YouTube and while the overdubbing is a little out, they are still amazing viewing 30 years on - yes, I have watched them all.

In one episode he would bash a certain tree bark which, when put in lakes, would starve the water of oxygen, meaning the fish would just float to the surface. Another episode saw him diving for lobster, but only catching one as the lobster emits a shriek that attracts sharks, so time was of the essence. It really was an amazing show and has given me a life-long fascination with foraging.

Later on, Ray Mears would do a similar series of shows, inspired by Les, his hero.

On top of Greek lessons therefore, I would also get lessons from Eirini on the plants and trees of Greece. As with Bush Tucker Man, there is so much food right in front of your nose, but only if you have the right knowledge. There are plants where if you collect the pink flowers and boil them it makes an antiseptic drink. Carob trees have pods that if you boil them down you can make a form of Nutella, something that kept the locals alive here during World War II. On top of that you have wild thyme, sage, mountain tea, oregano, fennel etc.

In just one walk through the mountains and by the beach, we gathered the following:

Clockwise from top left: Sea samphire, capers, caper flowers, wild fennel, mulberries, almonds, mountain thyme.

To harvest the olives, our team comprised me, a complete novice with a bad knee and a bad ankle, and a thirst for knowledge as I could use these techniques on our own trees, we had Eirini and also her brother, a kind and gentle beekeeper called Angelos. Angelos and Eirini had close to 100 years of olive harvesting experience between them, so were the perfect tutors.

Olive harvest under way: Eirini (L) and her brother Angelos (R).

We also had their mother, whom I call '*To Afentiko*' ('The Boss'). Eirini's mother is 89 and still very active with her amazing vegetable patch. She is a tough, friendly, yet formidable lady, who has stared down not one, but two firing squads in her lifetime. The first was in World War II and the second was during the Greek Civil War that followed. Whilst she took no side in the Civil War, she was taken prisoner by Communist soldiers and only saved from a firing squad by an injured Communist soldier whom she had been looking after.

Given the combined experience of my tutors, you would think that they ruled the show ... but you would be wrong. Eirini had warned me before that her mother loved to butt in and, sure enough, within three or four minutes she was there shouting at Angelos for cutting the wrong branch. It was hilarious. Everyone in Greece has their own way of doing it and everyone is right.

The technique is simple, yet would have taken me ages to work out myself. With the exception of the chainsaw, I doubt it has changed much in many, many centuries. First you lay overlapping nets around the tree and about 4m either side. One person does the cutting, in this case, Angelos with the chainsaw. Then two people - myself and Eirini - thrash the branches clear of all olives onto the mats. The thrashing is done with what is called a 'Rhythm Stick', which meant I had Ian Dury on my 'internal jukebox' all day. *#Hit me, hit me, hit me!#* Whilst it sounds like a fancy piece of kit, it is just a bamboo cane.

All branches with olives are cut, as olives won't grow for a second consecutive year in the same place, so space is made for new growth.

The harvest isn't just about collecting olives, it is also about preparing the tree for the next year and so any branches in the centre are also cut to give air flow for the next crop. The aim is to have a tree that looks like an upturned baseball glove or an upturned umbrella, with 3-5 'spokes' coming out from the tree.

Olive cutting is a competitive sport around here. My Albanian friend Luan ('the Lion') says that he can tell the nationality of the person who cut the tree and that the Albanians are the best. My Greek friends insist differently.

Larger logs are kept for fires the next year, after drying and seasoning, while the smaller branches are dried and used as goat food or kindling. On that note, perhaps the best cheap firelighter I have seen is a few sheets of kitchen roll soaked in olive oil, but pine cones do a similarly good job.

Once that tree is done you lift the sides of the net, pushing all the olives and leaves into the centre, then sort out the majority of the leaves from the olives. A small amount of leaves can be left, they are separated at pressing by a strong blowing machine.

Then once those olives are bagged, you move the nets around the next tree and start again.

It is backbreaking work. Despite my ailments I am fairly fit, I walk and swim lots. I did the day without much of a break and was absolutely shattered by the end. The next day I felt much like the first morning when you wake up after skiing or snowboarding. At a push I could have done another day or two, albeit in a lot of pain. Some people here, in fact most people here, do it for weeks or even months at a time. (A few Albanian friends of mine have a deal with Greek landowners whereby they tend the trees throughout the year and harvest the olives for a 50% share of the oil).

Lunch couldn't have come soon enough and it is one of those meals that I will never forget, not because it was Michelin starred, but because it was just … perfect. Everything about it was perfect.

To Afentiko prepared a large slab of fresh bread, olive oil on both sides instead of butter, fresh sliced tomato from her garden, large slabs of Kalavrita Feta (the best Feta) and herbs. Sat out under the freshly harvested trees still giving some shade, eaten in about three minutes - perfect.

How much oil you get from your harvest depends on a number of factors the age of the tree, the weather leading up to harvest (i.e. strong winds, no rain gives a poor harvest) and also the presence (or not) of the dacus fly.

Dacus, or Olive Fruit Flies, are relatively new here as far as I can tell, but they lay eggs in the olives and the larvae use the fruit for food. They can ruin entire crops. One friend who has about 110 trees got just 10% of the previous year's oil due to them. He told me that all we need are a few days of temperatures above 40 degrees and the fly is wiped out. We reach that and more most years, but not all years.

As an aside, the same friend drives a huge 3 litre gas-guzzling truck and pays less road tax than his wife's tiny Toyota car. Why? Because his 110 trees means he is technically a farmer and therefore he gets subsidised.

As a rough rule of thumb you get between 6:1 and 8:1, so six - eight kilos of olives gives you one litre of oil. That is before the pressing plant takes their 20% cut.

Yes, backbreaking work, but it must rank as one of my best ever days in Greece. Next year it will be our own olives from our own trees!

In mid-November we had the first of two large milestone celebrations in six months - celebrating being made redundant from my job, ten years previously. On that dark, cold day in London, I never thought that a decade later, I would be somewhere hot, celebrating that deeply distressing event.

Boy it was too, hotter than usual. Why?

… Because I decided to put on the very same suit, shirt and tie that I was wearing on that fateful day in 2009 … minus the shoes of course.

The year was rounded off with a fantastic meal at a friend's taverna, where we ate spit roast lamb and pork, chips and rice. All throughout the meal we were joined by a kitten with an absolutely filthy black and white coat. She looked malnourished and took full advantage of our extra large helpings of food. She was almost Maine Coon in style, unusual for an area where short haired cat dominate. We checked around and no one had seen her before. It was December and many street cats struggle to survive in winter and she was stick thin under the fur.

Meet cat number ten, Pepper (*Sgt Pepper, Pepperami, Pep Guardiola, Pep Squeak, Peps*).

Chapter Twenty Two - Things I Miss and Things I Don't Miss About the UK

I've already gone on at length about missing live music in the UK in a previous chapter, so I won't labour the point further. But I am often asked what it is I truly miss about the UK, and also what I don't miss at all, so here is a list, as always in no particular order.

1. Asian Food

Many Greeks don't care too much for hot and spicy food. Perhaps it is due to the fact that Greece has been a centre of emigration rather than immigration until recent turbulent times means that fewer nationalities have come to Greece, bringing their cuisine with them. Before 2021, in our village of maybe 30 tavernas, every single one is Greek food, with the exception of an Italian pizza place.

We do have a Chinese restaurant in Kalamata, but one hour is too far away for me.

I missed being able to browse through a menu, make a quick call and then 40 minutes later have 5 different curries in front of me to tuck into (a 'curry crescent'). Many tavernas do delivery here, but it's not a lot of use when you don't have an address.

Curry sauces in jars have made an appearance in supermarkets in recent years, plus poppadoms, so progress is being made. In 2021 a very good Indian restaurant opened down in the bay - you can just imagine my face upon hearing this news.

2. Choice in Supermarkets

When I go back to the UK, the supermarkets astound me. We have two great supermarkets with wonderful staff here, pretty much everything we need, but the range of food and drink compared to the UK is limited. I go back to the UK and see whole aisles devoted to ready meals, crisps, chocolate, orange squash etc and the aisles are packed from floor to ceiling.

3. Friends and Family

Yes, it is only 3.5 hours on a plane to Kalamata from London or Manchester and yes, Greece is an amazing country to visit, but still you don't see friends and family in any way near as much as you would like.

To the 'mere' 3.5 hours on a plane you have to add two hours for airport security, up to two hours to get to the airport, then at the Greek side you have to clear customs and wait for luggage - usually very swift - and then traverse up and down mountains for an hour to get to our house. It can easily therefore take up to nine hours to get here.

Off season, most flights to Kalamata stop and so to get here you have to fly into Athens, which is a four hour drive away, rather than the one hour from Kalamata.

Yes as well, this area is an amazing place to visit for all ages of the family, but almost all of my friends have young families and so are restricted by school holidays and a myriad of other demands. Well, it's either that, or they don't like me very much!

Even when we first moved out here, Anne's parents were too frail to make the journey, so our holidays used to involve going twice a year to live in Sunderland, where we had the guest suite at the sheltered housing unit.

It really was something of a turnaround. Back when we were working in London, we used to dream of holidays to far-off destinations in the sun - Greece always featured - and staying in fancy hotels. Now we lived in Greece we didn't want to leave our mountain, then we would fly to freezing, wet Sunderland and stay in the guest room at Anne's parents' sheltered housing complex - very comfortable and a bargain at £5 a night with free tea and coffee!

4. Pubs

I thoroughly enjoy a cold beer down at the beach, watching the sea and feeding the stray cats. In fact, I adore it. This isn't a moan, as I don't think they are comparable, but a nice pint in a pub after a cold winter walk is sorely missed. If on my own, maybe just sit in the corner and read Viz. Even better would be if the pub had bar snacks, a roaring log fire ... and even better than that would be a lazy pub dog or cat, snoring in front of the fire.

There really isn't anything more that I miss and to be honest, with the exception of friends and family, they aren't that important. I can cook pretty good curries now, the pub is balanced out by tavernas next to the sea and our supermarket stocks almost everything I want.

This isn't meant to knock the UK in any way, I am still fond of it, but there are, however, a large number of things that I really don't miss about it. In no particular order:

1. The Weather

Yes, it is incredibly obvious and predictable, but the weather in the UK was getting me down and had been for many years. We went through a period of heavy snow in winters towards the end of the first decade of this century and that meant having to take the Tube in, as riding Vespas in snow and ice is craziness. I *hate* the Tube. It's the reason I bought a Vespa in the first place.

The main problem was that the harsh winters didn't seem to be balanced out by nice summers, with a few lovely exceptions. I would book a holiday immediately after I came back from one and just counted down the days until I could be away again. That's no way to live - surely we could find a compromise?

2. The Commute

After Covid caused a 'work from home' regime for those people that could, many are probably realising now how much of a drag commuting actually is, and will be having the same thoughts that Anne and I did - is it worth the bother? It is costly, takes up valuable hours and quite frankly, who wants to be charged a fortune to be stuck on the Tube with your nose in some stranger's armpit?

I used to love our scooter rides in to work in London for the most part, but the roads are full of dangerous drivers and pedestrians have also nearly caused me many accidents. Once I was riding past what must have been the busiest bus stop in Camden when my front tyre hit some mud and slipped out beneath me. I was going at about 35mph, came off the bike and skidded 20 yards along the asphalt in front of 40 or 50 bemused commuters. A kind soul picked me up and checked I was OK and I was - I had no broken bones, more a massive sense of embarrassment and I got away from there as soon as possible. I hurt like hell for weeks and had a mark on my upper right thigh where my house keys scraped into me against the road.

Then when you get to your destination there is always a search for a parking bay. I started work earlier than most, but even then it was often very hard to find space. People would move bikes to get theirs in, leaving your bike a few inches over the line and so you are greeted with a £60 fine on your return. That happened at least 8 times. In ten years in Greece including several times in Athens and Thessaloniki and hundreds of times in Kalamata I have seen one, solitary parking warden. Greece is perhaps too far the other way compared with the UK; the Greeks love a bit of double or triple parking, or best still, the parking trick whereby you drive your car with the parking line down the middle of your car and stop when you are half way into the next space. This way just one single car can occupy four car parking spaces at one time.

Back in the UK there were, of course, glorious days of riding in lovely weather, watching the trees in the woods emerge from the winter into spring. July was even better due to school holidays. Empty roads, lovely scenery, perfect.

My commute now is down a flight of stairs, a quick pit stop at the kettle, then down a further flight of stairs; bedroom to office in three minutes.

4. People and Proximity

The UK is about 1.9 times bigger than Greece. Greece is approximately 131,957 sq km, while the UK is approximately 243,610 sq km.

However, the big difference is the population. The UK has approximately 66.7 million people, whereas Greece has just approximately 10.5 million people, however 3.2 million people live in Athens and 1.1 million people live in Thessaloniki, meaning that 40% of Greece's population live in just two cities.

Down in the Mani, our home, the population is multiplied by many times during tourist season, but year round most villages have several hundred people at most and land is plentiful.

In London we lived in a terraced maisonette and you could often hear what was going on next door or above and below you. Here, our nearest year round neighbour on our side of the road is 150m away to the right of us and … well, there isn't one on the left. The freedom is wonderful.

5. Work, Office Politics, 9-5

Strictly I didn't really work 9-5, it was more 7:30-12, lunch, 2-5. In my last job I had such an amazing bunch of colleagues whom I really miss, but there were people in another office who were the worst 'colleagues' you could imagine. The back stabbing and glory stealing was legendary. Success has many fathers and failure is an orphan. I really don't miss the political side of working in an office.

6. Crime

As I will sadly explain later, Greece is by no means crime free. But compared with London it is a dream. In 12 years of living in London my bike was stolen twice, vandalised countless times (20+) including cutting my fuel leads to get £5 of petrol on the day of my redundancy hearing, all four tyres on our car were slashed, my friend's handbag (wallet, keys, ID etc) was taken from our hallway using a pole and a hook through the letter box and next door was completely ransacked while our neighbour was away. They found her car keys, loaded up her car with all her valuables and then drove off.

It started to get me down, people making money out of our misery and at our cost.

7. Cost of Living

Houses in the UK were, and still are, at crazy prices. A generation of kids struggle to get on the housing ladder. In our area of Greece, €250,000 will buy you a three bedroom house with terrace, front and back garden and a sea view. That amount in London might just buy you a one bedroom flat. Maybe.

It's not just housing, but travel, eating out, drinking, taxis etc. Down in the village it is easy for two to eat out with starters, main course and a half litre of wine for €30 and prices haven't changed in ten years.

8. Politics

While we earn money in Sterling and have expenses in Euros and while the exchange rate remains poor as it has done since 2016, I have to keep an eye on UK politics, even more so with Brexit and our rights to continue to live in Greece. But I long for the day when none of that matters, when I can just ignore it all, where decisions made by people I don't believe have the capability to carry out their job, have no effect on me.

I follow Greek politics - it sure has been 'interesting' over the past ten years - and I have a rough idea of what is going on, but some day, one day, I can hopefully become blissfully ignorant of it all, both at home here and also in the UK.

Chapter Twenty Four: Common Mistakes People Make When Moving to Greece

I'd hate some of the many mistakes we made when moving out here to be repeated, so below, once again in no particular order, are the areas to take care with:

1. Buying a House Immediately

It is very easy to get carried away, especially when you have your 'UK' head on. Property prices in the UK are at such high levels now and so everything here seems like a bargain. If you buy immediately you are almost certain to buy in a location that you wouldn't have chosen two years later and you will almost certainly overpay, perhaps by as much as 30%; maybe even more.

We were lucky in so far as we didn't have the finances to buy immediately, we had to rent. In that time we discovered new areas and learned how the area changes over the year. It might seem a nice idea to live right near Stoupa bay, but for me the traffic and number of people at the peak of the season is too much. Having to regularly drive down the Kalogria Road in the middle of August is not something I would want to do.

Renting for a year or two means you can get to understand the local market much better, see what has been on the market for a while and what is good or bad value. More importantly, I bet that any house you would have bought on day one would not be the same house you would buy after two years.

2. Building

Perhaps this section should be retitled 'Building, or building without supervision'. It is the dream of many Brits to build their own house in the sun, but it isn't easy. The whole process will take up to 18 months and a Greek solicitor is essential - do not take one suggested by the builder, find one independently. The solicitor will then check that the land has proper title and isn't Forestry land, where building is prohibited.

Choose your land carefully. I know of people who have built their dream house only for the land in front to be sold a year later and their view lost. There are currently numerous houses being built near me and the noise for (too) many months has been immense. Ideally look for a piece of land that has no buildable land around it, or is already built on, but suitably private if that is your wish. Buying a house in the middle of olive groves might seem like a dream and indeed it may be, but it also has the possibility of tying you to a building site for the next 20 years as people consecutively build either side of you.

Make sure that your design includes a back-up water tank of at least 1000 litres, as the water supply has been getting increasingly erratic over the last few years with several areas having no supply for weeks.

Lastly, and most importantly, if you do decide to build, either be here to supervise it yourself or appoint someone to do so. Our house was built by a good local builder, but the previous owners who built the house left a large down payment and went back to the UK. The planning permission was for a two storey house with an underground basement, but when they came back six months later they found that the builder had decided to not dig into the rock, but just build up. They were the proud owners of a three storey house. Which was illegal. And he'd put in two extra bathrooms. And an extra kitchen. And now wanted €50,000 extra. This cost the vendors €7,500 to formally legalise before we purchased the house.

3. Life is Far More Simple than the UK

As mentioned earlier perhaps twice, when I first told a friend that I was moving to rural Greece, he asked 'won't you get bored?'

Of course the simple life is what most people come for, but sometimes in reality for some it is 'too' simple. I've had friends who missed the pub, missed their mates, missed the football, so much so that they have returned to the UK.

I haven't once been bored, but this life isn't for everybody.

4. Alcohol

It's a UK tradition to grab the outside tables at the pub on a sunny day. The difference is that for 7-8 months a year in Greece, *every* day is a sunny day. Wine is incredibly cheap, beer is very cheap. Perhaps you have retired or are working reduced hours, so you don't have to get up for work the next day. It is very, very easy to fall into the trap of drinking too much.

5. Family

Other than illness, the biggest single reason for people to return to the UK is because they miss their family. Grandchildren usually figure in the decision to return too.

We chose not to have children, but both sets of our parents have had serious illnesses and we have needed to be back in the UK regularly at different times of the year, sometimes at short notice. Kalamata airport is only open during the tourist season meaning a 4 hour drive to Athens is added to an already quite long journey. Keep family of all ages in mind when considering the move.

6. Work

I've heard of quite a few people who were thinking about moving here and then finding work to support themselves. Don't - it really isn't feasible without great contacts. Firstly, unemployment in Greece is high, especially amongst the younger generation. Secondly, when work is available, it will go to a family member or friend first. Lastly, from 1st January 2021 it became harder for British nationals to work in the EU. The salaries here are incredibly low as well compared to the UK.

There are a few examples of Brits who have found work, but they are mostly Greek speaking or people who have started their own businesses and employed other Brits.

Chapter Twenty Five: 2020 - An Anniversary and a Good Luck Sign that Brought No Luck.

Our first task of the year was to return to the UK and see Anne's mam. Her dementia had taken further hold, she had had a serious fall and it was desperately sad to see when we Facetimed her. I left Anne to do the arrangements and she booked us in to fly at the end of January.

We drove four hours to Athens and arrived at an airport we had grown very familiar with. Athens is a nice sized airport, you can walk from the car park to the airport, we knew where everything was and the gates were mostly quite near to the main hub. But one thing this year was very, very different.

We had been aware of reports coming from Wuhan in China about a new virus, Covid-19. By this time it hadn't been reported as having reached Europe, but perhaps in the fullness of time we would hear differently. Certainly, few in Europe were that worried, but I would estimate that 50% of people in Athens airport were wearing face masks, something that would perhaps become the single most identifiable symbol of what would turn out to be a pandemic, the worst to hit the UK since 1918.

On the plane I switched on my iPad to read the paper and then noticed the date: 31st January 2020. I was flying into the UK, via London Heathrow on the very day the UK was actually leaving the EU. There were street parties planned and the Leave.EU team had tried to get an under repair Big Ben to ring on the hour we left, a 'Big Ben Bong' - another one of these deeply annoying three word phrases that we would be constantly subjected to in coming months.

It felt like I was being trolled. The one day in 31 months that I didn't want to be in the UK and I would be staying the night in Sunderland, a place that had voted 61.3% to leave the EU. Sunderland had been the early warning sign that the Leave vote could indeed win. I just didn't get it, given that Nissan was the main employer in the area and they depended on just in time imports and access to the single market.

Over its history, Sunderland had endured two tragically devastating depressions - the end of ship building and the end of mining. It could be argued that these were the result of changing global dynamics, the rise of Asia as an economic powerhouse, but there is also a heavy political angle to the end of mining too.

It is hard to imagine today just how devastating these events were. As an example, my wife, Anne, left school in 1982 aged 16 and managed to get a job as an Admissions Clerk at Newcastle University. It was such an unusual occurrence that the news of her landing a job was announced over the school tannoy system.

As a sad economist, I read a lot about the regeneration of Sunderland, which occurred in the 1980s under the same Conservative government who were in control of the decision to end mining. One might argue that these were policies cruelly implemented many years too late by government, but I couldn't possibly comment.

They created large incentives for industries to relocate to the area, effectively giving away a huge 120 acre site of a former Royal Air Force base, with good road networks and close proximity to ports. I read the story of the man in charge of putting together the bid to get Nissan and others to move to the North East. He said that they rushed out to get one of these new inventions - *a word processor* - to type up the bid.

Don't bother buying one, they'll never catch on, kid.

Nobody knew how to use it, but they managed to grasp it quickly enough and they won the bid, bringing thousands of jobs to the area, not just to Nissan's factories, but to all of the ancillary firms that serviced the factory. The man leading the bid described hearing the news that they had won as the very best day of his life and rightly so - he had started the ball rolling of taking an entire region out of economic decline.

The two recent historical depressions were as a result of global economics and political decisions made down in Westminster. Now it seems likely that Sunderland is slowly heading for a third depression and this time it was due to votes from people living right there in the North East. This will be a depression of their own making and it was heart breaking to witness the very first hours of it.

I would so very much like to be wrong here, to have people tell me that everything I have said over five years turn out to be completely incorrect. I will have absolutely no happiness at being proved right - on this subject at least.

I saw the historic night in at the bar of the hotel we were staying in, watching a stupendously drunk man try and persuade people to come back to his house for a Brexit party, perhaps a metaphor. I declined his kind offer.

On arrival at Anne's Mam's nursing home, we were reminded about just what an amazing service she was getting - a kind welcome and an update on how she was doing. We were walked into the room where she was sat and she looked up.

'Hello our Dot!'

Dot is Anne's older sister.

'Who's he?'

'He' had been on the scene for 15 years now, 11 years as Jean's son-in-law.

Discussion was brief, it was hard. It was hard to see someone whom just 15 years previously I had desperately wanted, *needed*, to impress and gain the acceptance of, in such a bad way.

We stayed for two days, aware that this could be the last time that we spent with Mam.

On our return to our mountain we noticed a large amount of activity on our terrace. A pair of swallows had chosen to build their nest under the terrace roof and for two weeks they worked at a furious pace bringing back mud and grass to build an effective wattle and daub nest of approximately 8 inches in length.

Their work ethic was just amazing and I spent many an afternoon just watching them fly in, fix what they had in their beaks to the wall and then fly back out, only to be instantly replaced by their mate doing the same thing. Each round trip was approximately five minutes and they worked tirelessly from around 7am until 5pm.

Swallow returning to the nest it has built underneath our terrace

A friend told me that the Greeks believe that if swallows choose your house to nest in, it brings good luck - excellent, we could use a bit of that! I was also pleased to hear that the nests are protected by law and there are fines for anyone caught taking them down.

From our side, we were more than happy to have a couple of extra additions to our animal family and the swallows got used to us walking around on the terrace while they were at work, which is just as well, as the nest was only about 4 ft above our heads. We did question their choice of a house that had ten resident cats, but hoped that we could keep the two parties separate.

Not long after we noticed a small dappled egg shell on the floor under the nest and then the unmistakable sound of their young ... especially when food arrived. It seemed the poor parents had barely had a break from their arduous time constructing the nest before the young arrived and the next task of keeping them fed started, and so the hard work continued for our two fantastic parents, feeding their five youngsters.

Do you remember when 'Reet Petite' by Jackie Wilson which was re-released in 1987, together with a video of Plasticine figures, a bit like Morph from Take Hart from children's TV in the 1980s? I was constantly reminded of that when I saw those five baby hungry birds.

#Reet petite, The finest girls you ever wanna meet# [one baby hidden]

As the days passed, the five babies grew, yet the nest stayed the same size. Something was going to have to give and we desperately hoped that none of the babies would fall, as it was getting incredibly hard for them all to fit in. They ended up sleeping on each other, hanging over the sides, absolutely no social distancing whatsoever.

We could tell that it was soon time to flee the nest as each baby would perch on the side and practise flapping wings. With what was completely lucky timing, we were both around to video them leaving, one by one, first up onto a ledge a few metres from the nest where they were safe from feline attacks, and then all five out into the real world.

It was utterly, utterly joyful to witness. On top of that, I am told that adults return to the same nest year on year, so we should hopefully have our two back next year. Logically they should, I mean really, who would want to build a new nest every single year? We shall wait and see.

With the 'B' word implementation date fast approaching I needed to do some final preparation. I had been a holder of temporary residency card for Greece for five years and that allowed me to exchange the current beige/buff card for a blue Permanent Residency card.

This means going to a Police Station with a whole binder of documents, originals and copies, and asking them to issue the card.

It really isn't as easy as it should be. For a start, the police - perhaps understandably - are fed up with having to issue so many cards. Secondly, they don't believe that British people need Permanent Residency cards; that the buff Temporary card will do. But having Permanent Residency gives you more protection than the Temporary card and given the constantly evolving political situation I wanted to do absolutely every single thing that I could to secure our lives here.

I know of quite a few British people living here or with holiday homes here who don't even have the buff Temporary card. There was a window to get this which closed on 1st January 2021 and will not ever open again. Those without either the Temporary or Permanent cards will only be able to spend up to 90 days here in any 180. That makes holidays difficult as many like to spend months continually here and it also makes permanent residency impossible without a specific visa or a Golden Visa, both difficult to obtain.

The real kicker that many people do not yet understand fully is that those 90 days in any 180 apply to *all* Schengen countries, so you could theoretically come and spend 80 days in Greece, but if you had recently spent a fortnight in France you would be in breach of the rules and liable for a nasty fine. It has been indicated that fines will be fairly steep, a second offence would be an even steeper fine and a third offence could mean jail, but we will see how that plays out.

It is quite the process - I have known people turned away five, six, seven times as they didn't have the right documents. There is an official list of documents that are needed, but it is very common for the police to ask for something completely different and if you don't have it then you get turned away again. They even asked for a translated copy of our marriage certificate for Anne's card.

'Why is your marriage certificate in English?'

'Erm ... because we got married in London?'

You basically have to take every single official document - copies of each - plus the kitchen sink.

My first attempt ended in failure - I didn't have copies of my tax returns for five years. They gave me a piece of paper with a list of everything I needed and told me to make a new appointment. I looked at the list - I had everything! Tax returns, according to their very own list, weren't required. So I went back in and told them I had everything on their list and they just said 'yes, you also need tax returns for five years'. I told you it wasn't straightforward.

I decided that I needed help as while my Greek was conversational it wasn't yet at the point where I could have a debate with someone, especially someone who didn't want to give me something that I wanted and needed. My friend Eirini was my first choice - intelligent, calm, reasonable and yet capable of being the fiercest thing you have ever seen if required; the perfect ally.

The second time, again they really didn't want to issue the card, they said it was fine as it was, Temporary. Eirini calmly explained the position and I believe made a few calm threats and then finally there it was - my blue Permanent Residency card for the Hellenic Republic of Greece. No getting rid of us now! One slight snag was that I had forgotten to photocopy one document, out of a huge binder of documents. They made me go back to the village to photocopy it when there was a photocopier just a few metres from us. It was a petty display of power, but who cared? I had what I needed, I had our extra security.

One morning in spring we came down to find a window open on the ground floor. We had been in that room the previous day and must have forgotten to close it, which was silly. As I have mentioned before a couple of times, crime is thankfully very rare here, but most summers there are a spate of robberies. We checked for valuables - not that we really have any - and everything seemed fine. Laptops were still in the office, car keys and car all present, so we didn't think anything of it.

Then we got a call from our neighbour, who was back in the UK at the time. I was watering her garden and another neighbour was feeding her cats, who were locked in at night. At about 11:15pm our neighbour spotted one of the cats by his window - he was sure he locked them away. He went to her house and checked - there had been a break-in. The robbers had prised open one of her windows, scared the cats who then ran to his house, alerting him. They had gone by the time he arrived, but had opened the safe and made off with quite a bit of cash.

As soon as she told us she had been burgled we went back down to the window that we thought we had left open and looked at it with fresh eyes - they had tried to rob us too.

Both of us were in bed at the time, well asleep, and so we can only think that Floyd had heard them and scared them off as nothing had been taken.

The police were called and they explained that these gangs don't want to rob holiday houses for a TV or a kettle, they wanted occupied houses with wallets, car keys, iPhones, iPads, cash. We think that our neighbour had been unfortunate because she had been given a lift to the airport by friends and left her car outside, potentially indicating that she was still in the house, when in fact she was a few thousand kilometres away.

I'm sure most people reading this have been robbed before, and it is a most unsettling feeling. The objects taken can mostly be replaced, with the exception of sentimental items, but it is just more the fact that people have been in *your* house. What if they had been armed and we had disturbed them? How long had they been watching us?

I'd experienced a burglary before, but that was in my student house in Birmingham. That was also deeply unsettling. Worse still, it took us eight hours to realise we had been burgled and ransacked as the place was such a mess. Sure, the door was hanging off its hinges, but that was normally due to my drunk housemate forgetting his keys.

It cost us €500 to replace the window that they had prised open, which was a rather unwelcome bill, given that we were furloughed from work. The window was just 15 ft below the recently vacated swallows' nest - not the good luck we had been promised, sadly.

Ah yes, 'furlough' - a word I had never heard before 2020 and I suspect one that much of the population hadn't heard before either.

Covid-19 had steadily spread to Europe, with Italy and Spain experiencing early spikes. The UK was sadly to follow, in fact the very first case in the UK was recorded when we were visiting Anne's Mam in January/February.

Our work had dried up and we were placed on furlough, meaning 80% of the previous average salary of the previous year - a very bad year for us financially, so 80% of 'not a lot'.

To cheer ourselves up, we took Floyd down to Kalogria beach for a swim and for a meal at a favourite taverna, one that served amazing food, with a great view and had two taverna kittens to fuss. I still remember it well: fried taleggio cheese with orange marmalade, a rocket salad with shaved parmesan, rusks and dried figs to start, pastitsio for Anne, grilled pork belly and chips for me.

Kalogria Beach, March 2020

We chatted with the waiter about life in general and he expressed his worry about the virus and how it might affect the tourist season.

The next day, March 23rd 2020, Greece went into full lockdown, way in advance of many other countries and, with hindsight and looking at the statistics, a very good call.

To leave the house we would now have to either fill in a form or get SMS authorisation and could only leave to walk the dog, go to the pharmacy, go food shopping or visit the doctor. You would have to carry this form on you at all times, together with a passport and residency card.

We had effectively already self-isolated for a decade, plus we had outside space unlike many others. We had each other, we had the animals and most importantly, we had Greece.

THE END

I HOPE YOU ENJOYED THIS BOOK AS INTENDED: A LOVE LETTER TO GREECE - THE COUNTRY AND ITS PEOPLE.

Chapter Twenty Six: 2020 - Thought You'd Got Rid of Me? Well, Unfortunately For You, Like Backstreet ... I'm Back!

I originally thought official lockdown in Greece, would be a perfect day to end the book.

Although I discussed it in the previous chapter, we were ten days short of our tenth anniversary of arriving in Greece in an over-packed car driven through Europe. We had made a huge amount of progress, we had also suffered setback after setback and had a rough ride from time to time, set against the most beautiful backdrop one could imagine.

A new way of life had descended on Greece that day and for many other countries too. Some, as we would later learn, had locked down sooner than others. Many countries were affected in different ways, some had huge death tolls, some were small, but still too big to bear. Some were prepared, others weren't at all and some even denied the exact scale of the problem that they were facing. Some had people ready to face the challenge ahead in charge, others sadly did not. Others had politicians ready to plunder public finances, either for their own pocket, or for those of their friends and backers.

As I look at my scruffy notebook, I can see that these notes were scrawled on 9th November 2020, Χαλάνδρι (Chalandri), Athens, sat on a fairly uncomfortable chair writing on a pad, until the pain of the cannula, roughly pierced into my hand, got too bad and then I thought it best to stop and just wait to be called.

Yes, shit got bad, then it got good, then it got bad again not long after.

The good is too good to not tell you - perhaps the thing I am most proud of in my life - the bad just needs to be faced up to and told honestly. Both are linked in the most bizarre way.

Please read on?

Chapter Twenty Seven: 2020 - Has It *Really* Been TEN Years!?

Greece is in lockdown. It is a harsher lockdown than many countries in the world, including the UK.

But what exactly did it mean? For a start, all tavernas, cafés, bars, shops were shut. There were exceptions of course - you could go to the doctor, hospital, certain stores such as supermarkets or food shops, pharmacies etc. You could also exercise, be it alone, or with your pets.

Other than that you were expected to stay at home.

If you left the house, you had to carry a mountain of documentation on you - firstly either send an SMS text confirmation, or you had to fill in a paper form containing six options (referring to what you were doing), add your address (we don't have one!), sign it etc, carry your passport and Residency Card at all times. I don't have a mobile phone and so the SMS system didn't quite work for me. I had kept my Blackberry from work, issued in 2005, after redundancy and once got it out on a plane to call Anne when we had landed, only for a whole row of teenagers to laugh at me and how outdated it was. It will be back in fashion in about five years I reckon, perhaps like me.

Floyd would go crazy at the beginning of lockdown as I would get the dog lead out first and she would be all excited … only to wait for 15 minutes of bureaucracy and form filling before a nice stroll in the olive groves.

I should point out that the above is just to inform people of what the laws were here. I didn't have a problem with it. A law is a fairly blunt instrument, meant to cover all situations. It covers people in the centre of Athens and Kalamata, but its relevance to a bloke, his wife and his Border Collie on a sparsely populated mountain, many kilometres from any conurbation of over 500 people is a moot point.

That said, I complied 100% - unless I forgot! I have a fair few acquaintances who sadly believe that this pandemic is a government conspiracy, *blah blah blah*, Bill Gates and did I mention George Soros and them tracking you wherever you go? Please.

There is a theory that fits perfectly here I think, called Hanlon's Razor. Essentially it states *'never attribute to malice that which can adequately be explained by stupidity'*. In other words: *'before you cry conspiracy, first rule out incompetence'*. Governments *are* corrupt, we all know that - just see the current UK Conservative Government who are rotten to the core - but do you honestly think they are competent enough to carry out a conspiracy like this? Sure, the UK government managed to stagger Brexit across the line - just, with more issues to come - but even the sun shines on a dog's arse every once in a while.

I worked with statistics for my entire career, they can be manipulated however people would like, to a certain degree. I have certain doubts about the overall Covid death figures and statistics - particularly intra-country statistics that cannot be compared - but the two conclusions for me (just a sad economist with no scientific training) at the time were very simple:

1. Covid is real, it is a massive threat and it mutates.
2. The actions of government - wherever in the world - are crucial. Look at NZ versus the UK.

In the first wave, the Greek government did well versus many others and figures were mercifully low. Most people were OK. New Zealand was the poster child for the response, but Greece wasn't far behind. Most people here were really behaving. The government was well ahead of a population that was looking to get around the rules.

I've written before about my admiration for the Greek spirit of 'sod this, why don't we just try this instead?' and I must admit that it is one of the reasons I have stayed here.

The new Covid restrictions came in before Greek Easter. Unless you have experienced a Greek Easter you just don't know how amazing it is. It is the biggest and most popular holiday of the year. Christmas,

New Year, even Assumption in mid-August just do not compare. It is families together at their villages of birth all around the country, huge parties, spit-roast lamb, drinking, dancing, shooting of guns, fireworks … it really needs to be experienced. I adore it.

Bear in mind that almost half of Greece lives in two cities - Athens (fairly central) and Thessaloniki (NE) -and you have crazy migration around the country for this celebration.

A medical expert might say that in this year, 2020, this migration was not helpful and so the Greek Government took measures to stop it, in ways that made me respect them even more (bear in mind this government in Greece was the very rough equivalent of the Conservative Government in the UK, a government that - in polite terms for this book - I don't have a huge amount of respect for).

One of many of the Greek traits that I loved, that felt like I was born with, was to show respect for authority when it was warranted - *of course* - but also a disrespect for authority when it was forced on you for no reason. Respect needs to be earned in all walks of life. Just because you are more senior than another person in a job for example doesn't mean you are better than them. Prove why you are, help them, teach them, explain difficult things, cover for them even. That is how respect is earned. The Greeks I know completely understand this.

It was now Easter 2020 and Greece was in lockdown. I cannot understate the importance of Easter here and I adore it in usual times. Many Greeks will travel for hours and hours to get to their village of birth or their familial village. Families meet up, have feasts, drink dance etc, everything that I told you before, but with added guns and fireworks. It is so much fun.

But not in 2020. The Greek government didn't want Covid spreading and they decided to stop anyone moving between prefectures. It made sense, but this meant families not meeting up. That said, this is Greece - there must be a way around it?

It was reported that some Greeks changed their ID cards to state that their home address was their familial village, which meant that they couldn't be stopped on the main motorway toll booths. Much of the motorway system, at least from Athens down here to the Mani, is toll roads. It makes it very easy for the police to stop people. That said, they are the easiest roads that I have ever driven on - empty, amazing scenery, almost like someone driving up the M1 in the 1950s in the UK. The 4 hour journey from Athens down to Kalamata costs about €15 in tolls, there are loads of great service stations, it really is a fantastic journey.

I watched in disbelief as the UK government struggled to deal with the Covid threat on so many levels. It was incompetence personified and the figures sadly speak for themselves.

Back when Anne and I and the cats arrived in May 2010 some of my English friends - plus perhaps my parents - were questioning our decision, saying Greece looked like it was a mess. Yes it was - financially - but the UK looked like it was losing all control of things just ten years later, while Greece was relatively fine.

Greece had a government that recognised the threat early and a government that acted early. Bear in mind, just four years previously, Vote Leave won a referendum to take the UK out of the EU on the promise to *'take back control of our borders'*. During this period, Greece - a sovereign nation, but part of the EU - actually *closed* part of its borders at points, as did other sovereign European nations. The UK kept its border open *throughout* the pandemic and at the time of writing *still* has them open.

If ever there was a time to 'take back control' and to close UK borders, that surely was it - and what did they do? Absolutely nothing.

It felt strange. I am typing this in August 2021 and it looks like Kabul will fall to the Taliban very soon after the UK/US left Afghanistan. I didn't have any interest in politics until the 9/11 attacks and the subsequent invasions of Afghanistan and Iraq. It is trite, I admit it, but I was not a student who would go on marches, I just wanted to go clubbing, I didn't take much notice of global or even domestic politics.

9/11 changed that, aged 27. I felt anger at the US administration trying to blame Iraq for this. I wasn't sure how long an intervention in Afghanistan would last, or what its effectiveness would be.

The reason for the last few paragraphs is to explain that I was never really political … until I was.

The next milestone was Brexit, in 2016. Just like the Iraq War (or 'Operation Freedom' as they felt it right to call it), Brexit had a surplus of serious misinformation, a (slim) majority, the support of both major political parties … and it passed. Can you show me someone who still thinks that the invasion of Iraq and the subsequent creation of ISIS in a US prison camp was a good idea?

So it felt really strange to be sitting in Stoupa in 2020, in the midst of a pandemic, actually admiring a government that I live under, for the first time in 19 years. The government we have are the very rough equivalent of The Conservative Party in the UK , the ones who were giving out lucrative PPE contracts to their mates through a 'VIP Lane' and who presided over one of the worst death tolls per 100,000 of population in the entire world.

The Greek government was so forward looking and had such an understanding of its population that it actually anticipated that some people would change their ID cards to say they lived in their birth village, just so they could attend Easter with their family! Police were told to enforce the rule about not crossing prefecture lines and the media were briefed that anyone trying this trick would have to stay in their birth village rather than return to Athens or Thessaloniki!

Enough politics, how did the Mani do during the pandemic? Tavernas were allowed to do takeaways and deliveries, they had to adapt, as did their customers, but it obviously wasn't the same. I know I speak for a number of people here, but a lovely long lunch at a taverna by the sea is one of life's pleasures, but that just couldn't happen.

Lockdown was gradually lifted in stages, each time we were given a bit more freedom.

The Greek Tourism Minister was incredibly positive - but of course, that is his job. I would guess that it is his choice, combined with the PM and the Chancellor as to when to open up. That must be the worst job in the world, you just cannot win - there are only shades of losing.

On the one hand you lock down 100% and that should probably stop infections in the population, assuming the population complies. But that kills the local economy without a doubt. Stoupa is probably 80% reliant on tourism, the rest being olives and construction.

This money flows around the economy in a way that a sad economist (like me) would call 'the multiplier effect': I spend €1,000 in a taverna (which I could give a damn good try at if you gave me a few hours). The taverna owner then has a marginal propensity to consume of, say, 0.9. That means the bar owner next door gets a nice €900 from the thirsty taverna owner. Then the bar owner needs some new tables and he has a much lower marginal propensity to consume of 0.4 and so he spends €360. You get the idea.

It is like throwing a stone in the sea - your action causes many others to automatically happen, like a ripple effect.

The whole thing is circular, with one exception: outflows. Imagine if Thomas Cook owned a load of hotels or villas, the profits there would be sucked back into a (now) bust corporation based in the UK or somewhere else. But that doesn't happen here, almost everything is family owned, which is why it is all the more important that money is spent here, so it stays here. The circular flow of money stays local, which is fantastic.

On the other hand we still had numerous Covid cases, but our part of Greece at the time of writing has managed relatively well.

Us personally? We've already been kind of self-isolated for ten years, it was a breeze.

We had planned on a good celebration on 1ˢᵗ May 2020, however. It was the tenth anniversary of arriving in Stoupa, having driven across Europe in a packed car.

TEN YEARS. TEN YEARS.

I remember having a line that I had worked out when people were speaking to me at our leaving party. I had no idea what we were doing, neither did Anne, I didn't want to walk back with my tail between my legs a few years later, having been all bullish on it, so I just said 'We are off to Greece and we both really hope it works out'.

TEN YEARS. TEN YEARS.

We did it. Somehow.

We sat in the field, surrounded by spring flowers, chickens, cats and Floyd. It was perfect. Our lovely French neighbours had given us a bottle of champagne from the vineyard at the bottom of their French house in exchange for jump starting their car to escape lockdown and it was wonderful. If they had been an hour later for that ferry they would have been stuck here for months.

Yeah, it wasn't how we planned it, but it was still a wonderful day amongst all the downsides of lockdown.

It was a time for reflection, remembering things that we had forgotten happened to us, until one of us piped up, a time to ruminate on just how naïve and occasionally stupid we were. We both spoke fluent French and yet instead of moving to the South of France as we had originally planned to do, moved to Greece, where we couldn't even say 'thank you' on arrival.

It was a time to remember who we had lost along the way [Jack, Spankie, Marley, Sparky and Franklin], but it was also a time to remember just what we had achieved and that was a real net positive. Not only had we moved 2,130 miles from home [by road], moved away from all our friends and family, we had actually managed to work out the landscape, know the right people to get whatever we needed done, read and speak the local language and get residency after Brexit.

Our trips to the UK had been almost all family related. We had watched Anne's Mam, Jean, deteriorate from almost the minute Jack died. We suspected she had been suffering from dementia for a while before, but immediately after Jack passed her faculties plummeted. Anne's sister, Dot, had taken most of the strain, but the care home was now telling us that Jean was at 'end of life stage'.

Jean died on 31st May 2020, the morning of her 92nd birthday, in her care home near Sunderland. We were all heartbroken, but there was also a sense of reality and, yes, relief. She had no quality of life and she didn't even recognise her own family.

Her funeral was held in the exact same place as her beloved Jicko. The only difference was the venue now only allowed 10 guests, all socially distanced due to Covid.

Anne and I watched the funeral on the internet from Greece, as there was no chance of travelling to the UK at the time. I'm guessing that most of the people reading this have all watched an internet funeral by now. The world is changing, just not in the way I would like it. That was 'a first' that was not an enjoyable experience, although our Dot put in a great speech, the service was very moving, but we were not there as we should have been. I have read this same thing thousands of times from other people. Not being there to say goodbye to your nearest and dearest is utterly heart breaking.

Once lockdown lifted, we had a mildly busy summer in 2020. There were lots of Greeks coming down here, fewer English. August - always a crazy month - was the most crazy I have ever seen it.

At one point we had three sets of friends out at the same time, some staying with us and some down in the village.

I had been getting daily headaches, for weeks now. They weren't as bad as the awful migraines I had when I was younger, aged 11-15, but I had to lie down in a quiet, dark room. Normal painkillers weren't working and the builders across the gorge were drilling into the rock constantly from 8am-4pm. I went to see my amazing Doctor in the village, Sofia. She told me to get an eye test (done, passed, but I still need glasses) and an MRI.

An MRI is a weird thing. You are basically stuck in a metal tube for about 30 minutes, listening to techno music. You cannot move. I am utterly claustrophobic, so much so that when I was a kid I used to ruin things when my brother and I would hide from Mum before bedtime - I always had to have my head poking out from under the bed.

But, as with needles that would almost make me faint at one point in my life, my stupid messed up body and stupid illnesses would mean that I would endure countless episodes of both, so that they are now as usual as making a cup of tea.

The Greek word for an MRI is '*Magnitiki*' which makes sense given that it is magnet based. You lie down on the 'tray' and are given a panic button to press if you need to use it. Given I was having a scan of my brain, they needed me to keep my head as still as possible, so I was packed into what looked like a Stormtrooper helmet, with foam padding all around my head.

I couldn't help but be amused, as my Aunt and Uncle had actually made the original Stormtrooper suits for Star Wars. They even had a full piece Stormtrooper suit in their living room, which was pretty damn cool for an 8 year old me to see. My Aunt later sold it as an original on eBay and collected a pretty penny or two from a Japanese collector.

None of my friends at school believed me when I told them - and oh boy, could I tell you much more if I and my family had immunity from prosecution - and they started singing along to what I think was a Steve Wright in the afternoon jingle 'It's another true story', but replacing the word 'true' with 'Guy'.

'It's another Guy story!'

When my brother got married I had a lot of fun putting my Aunt on 'the doubters' table. I still never received an apology, but perhaps that is because I expanded my repertoire of 'stories' to include one that I still think is true - my great grandad invented the phrase 'I'm alright, Jack'. He was also General Secretary of Sinn Fein and was best friends with Michael Collins, fighting the English in 1918 (this one is true!).

On occasion I went too far, just testing the boundaries of what I could get away with. I claimed my grandfather invented the question mark and I would like to apologise for that one. I nicked it from Mike Myers in the Austin Powers film I think. Anyway, I will have to change that story now I live in Greece as the question mark is actually a semi-colon. This is not the final Mike Myers reference in this book, however.

I got out of the MRI and said to the Doctor: *'I think I went to techno clubs in Birmingham like that in 1994 - the drugs were waaaaay better back then though'.*

We said goodbye to our last guests for the year in late September. We adore having people over - please come you lot! - but also we need to detox afterwards, fasting up to four days a week, no booze. I can't believe what I used to eat and drink in London. Over the last 18 months after my employer went bust, we would show up at 9am (previously 7:30am) on selected days - I managed 3 a week - and on those days by about 9:10am it would be 'so where are we going for lunch?'

It would be lunch at ten minutes before midday, two hours or so, maybe longer. We could have written a guide to the area as we went everywhere, just waiting to be made redundant. A personal favourite was the Golden Hind, pretty much at the bottom of Marylebone High Street. It was a fish and chip shop established in the first year of WW1. It was unlicensed so you could nip into the Nicholas Wine Shop and get a few bottles of chilled white wine then eat the most amazing fish and chips.

Wow, I am sure that the quality is still just as good … but looking at their website now I see their prices have gone up by 100% in the decade since I last ate there!

They say don't tempt fate. We've done it a few times and it has bitten us on the arse in a really bad way. Whenever of late we have said 'well, what *else* can go wrong?' everything has gone wrong.

This should never, ever be asked.

As an example: I made a rare trip back to the UK in 2015 to attend the funeral of my best mate from University, Harry-Krish Mootoosamy. It still hurts now and I still think about that dude every single day, his gentle, funny nature … and the stuff we used to get up to is best told face to face. My partner in crime, taken from his wife Asha and their three children, his family, his multitude of friends, and me, aged 39. We got to the venue and there were so many people that maybe 80% of the attendees had to stand outside and listen from speakers. That is how loved that man was. I stood outside in the rain, wind and sunshine - the world threw all it had at us - and honoured my friend.

We left without really speaking to anyone as I was too upset, and within five minutes, our tenant in London rang up with a problem - her cat sitter had locked the keys in the flat and couldn't get in, and the tenant was in the US. My problem? We got the spare keys around from a friend, but the keys had been changed the month before and not updated - all of this while driving up the A1 in floods of tears.

Anne then uttered the immortal - and never to be repeated words - 'what else could go wrong?'

Within five minutes, the mobile rang. It was my Aunty Cathy who had meant to arrive the day before at our house in Greece to house-sit and feed our cats … but who hadn't arrived. More stress, thinking an accident had happened as 29 calls remained unanswered.

Well she now had arrived, but the ground floor of the house had flooded - where were the stop cocks and is there a plumber you could call please?

You would have thought this would have taught both Anne and I that saying things like that do not bring positive outcomes?

But I managed to tempt fate that day in September 2020, when I said that the rest of the year was going to be a doddle - *'Anne, the next date in the diary is September 2021, let's just enjoy a relaxing six months , no work, no guests, nothing, just us and the animals'.*

The very next day our wonderful village doctor, Sofia, emailed me and asked me to come down to discuss my MRI results. Perhaps naively I just drove down there without a care in the world. Why would I have a care? I was just 47, in relatively good health, what's to worry about?

As was pretty usual for our village doctor I waited just ten minutes to be seen, no appointment necessary. I sat down at Sofia's desk.

'Yieassou Guy, I have your MRI results. I am afraid to say that you have a brain tumour'.

What the ....?

I heard the words, I just didn't have any idea what it meant, but luckily Sofia put me right. She told me that if one was in a thoroughly ideal world and *had* to 'choose' to have a tumour, they would choose mine. Why?

1. It was non-malignant. This is the game changer. If a tumour is malignant it takes things to another level, one where you really don't want to be. Mine was non-cancerous.

2. It was small-ish (we will come back to that point later).

3. It was in the right frontal lobe, which is the best for operations. Some unlucky people have tumours at the back of the head, around ear level and that makes surgery far more difficult.

4. I had insurance. The *chiselling weasels* didn't pay up when I was in the hospital in Athens in 2016, but maybe they would this time.

Doctor Sofia told me that she would ring around her friends to find the best consultant in Greece for me and, true to her word as always, gave me the contact details later that day of a consultant/surgeon in Athens.

I have to laugh right now because I am typing this a week away from my next MRI to find out if this treatment was successful. The book was done, finished a year ago. But I decided to add a few updates and I am looking at my scrappy notebook with my awful handwriting and I was documenting this in Athens In October 2020, immediately before the treatment that would hopefully rid me of this unwelcome guest in my cranium.

I was waiting in the hospital, not for long, jotting down notes for the things you have just read above and then was called in to the treatment room. They had to give me an injection for a procedure that I will later explain in all its gory glory - 'gory glory', I rather like that!

The scrawled message in my notebook just read 'CANNULA IN! CAN'T WRITE!'

For those of you lucky enough to not have visited many hospitals, a cannula is something that they put into your vein, usually in your hand, so that they can easily hook you up to what medicine they want to give you, either by syringe or by drip. I had one in my right hand for the entire stay at the clinic in Athens in summer 2016. There they hooked me up to a drip for 3 hours or more a day. In Athens, they had something else in mind, but I will come to that later.

Doctor Sofia set me up with an expert on brain tumours in Athens. To travel there we had to have written confirmation of the appointment and proof that it was for medical reasons, as due to the Covid lockdown we were not allowed to travel between prefectures.

It was lovely being back in Athens - what a city - and by absolute chance, we were staying right near a really good Indian restaurant. I say chance, but as I am sure you have guessed, there was absolutely no chance involved whatsoever. God bless the internet.

Our hotel was almost immediately beside the US embassy - perhaps not ideal - but was lovely. One of the less tragic casualties of Covid was the demise of the hotel buffet breakfast. Who doesn't love a hotel buffet? Fill your plate up, then go back again in 10 mins for a repeat performance. The best thing about Greek hotel buffets is that they always include cake as well, usually lemon cake and Madeira cake. I asked a Greek friend why this was and she said that the Greeks are so obsessed with bitter coffee, which has to be taken with something sweet, hence the cake (or '*keik*' as the Greeks say).

All you can eat hotel breakfast buffet with cake? Count me in.

But this story doesn't have a sad ending - far from it. Instead of the buffet, you were given a 2 sided piece of A4 paper with everything that the buffet had. Want bacon? Just tick. Eggs? Tick. We ticked most of both sides - there was even Bougatsa, which is the most amazing desert, originating in Thessaloniki - spiced filo pastry filled with custard. Seriously, don't try one, they are too good.

Free rein in a hotel buffet with no one judging you for your third visit AND all delivered to your room? I think we ordered some fruit too.

The consultant was amazing - relaxed, exact and factual, just what you want in these situations. The hospital was a 5 minute walk from our hotel and once we were temperature checked we were allowed in.

The consultant saw us bang on time, which was wonderful, as you could imagine. A 3-4 hour wait would have been torture.

We went to his office and he reviewed my MRI scans. The news really wasn't good. In fact it was pretty horrible. If you are particularly squeamish I suggest you forward on to the next set of paw prints.

The consultant said that my tumour was most probably too big to be dealt with by laser therapy, radiology, basically radiation pumped into my head. He had a friend, also in Athens that he would check with, as radiology was by far the best option. But I was previously told my tumour was small? It was 2.6cm to be precise, and had been growing for 6-8 years approximately. Think of it as a very unwanted 40th birthday present, from my body to me.

If the tumour was too big for laser therapy, what was probably needed was one Frankenstein of an operation:

1.   Drill in and cut out a quarter of my skull.

2.   Extract the tumour.

3.   Keep the quarter of the skull in a laboratory in Athens for FOUR months. FOUR MONTHS? This is so the doctors can

scrape off the tumour cells so that it will not reappear at some later date.

4. Walk around with just 75% of my cranium for four whole months.

5. Reunite my cranium with its old friend four months later.

Both operations would involve at least 2 days in ICU, then a week in 'normal' hospital.

The consultant was brilliant, he was the kind of professional that I like - he dealt in cold, hard facts, no matter how unpleasant they are to hear. He refused payment too! I don't know why, but I wasn't having that, no matter how lovely the gesture. I put a €50 on the table and he insisted I take it back. Well, we were staying next to an amazing Indian restaurant!

As we walked back from the hospital we heard a huge amount of noise. There was one hell of a demonstration going on and we didn't know why. We were very near Syntagma Square, where the Greek Parliament sits, scene of some disturbance in 2010/11.

We got back to the hotel, turned on the news and in our rudimentary Greek we understood what was going on, just a block away from us. There had just been a ruling that the 'political party' Golden Dawn was no longer a 'political party', but a criminal organisation.

Golden Dawn was the equivalent of the National Front in the UK - far right, anti-immigration, racist thugs. They had approximately 12% of the Greek vote at one point, but to put this into perspective, far right groups in many European countries have had far higher polling records, France and Hungary being prime examples.

There was a Golden Dawn office in our nearest city, Kalamata, above one of my favourite burger joints. Their flag, an appropriation of the Swastika, flew proudly above.

So, we have established that unfortunately far right parties are firstly in existence in Europe, but they are also doing quite well. But how many people reading this can say that they saw on television their far right politician punching a woman on a live show? Yes, that sadly happened in Greece!

The Golden Dawn Spokesman, Illias Kasidiaris, was on a panel with left wing politicians and got into a heated debate. He threw a glass of water over one of the other panellists, which was fairly tame compared with what came next. He was ex-Greek Special Forces (a step up from the usual National Service) and also a weightlifting enthusiast.

Another panellist, Ms Kanelli, made a few points that managed to annoy him so much, that he slapped her around the face three times. He then went on the run. I've never seen a Question Time episode with that drama before.

Chapter Twenty Eight: Three Is The Magic Number. Yes It Is, It's The Magic Number.

Can you imagine driving for four hours after being told you would lose 25% of your cranium for four months and have to spend weeks in hospital?

No, I couldn't really then, I am not sure that I can really now. It seems to be a sequence of events:

1.   You get told the news.

2   You immediately know it is bad, but cannot process just how bad it is.

3.   A few hours later you understand and realise just how bad it is.

4.   Then you start to think of the implications.

5.   Can I work? Will I just be bed-bound? What are the long term implications of this?

6.   Will it involve numerous treatments?

7.   How bad will the scars be? Pretty bad I would guess. And where?

8.   What if it goes wrong? They are drilling into my HEAD! I will be in ICU during Covid!

As we drove home I said to Anne, 'this has been a rotten day, I deserve beer'.

We got home and I wanted a walk to clear my head, so I took Floyd with me to the local shop, about a 10-15 minute walk away.

At the end of our road are some communal bins. They get emptied every 2-3 days which is great. But the bins attract a lot of stray cats looking for scraps. For the last 11 years, Anne and I have fed the stray cats in the region. It is my indulgence, my luxury, my replacement for not going out for lost weekends in London and it gives me the best thrill ever. The strays all have names and we have adopted one or two. Well, perhaps a few more than that.

I wandered past in a foul mood and heard an unusual sound. It wasn't the sound of a mature cat, more of a squeal. It was repeated and so I tracked it down to a plastic Jumbo bag - Jumbo is a shop in Kalamata selling mostly cheap Far Eastern made plastic toys and household goods, which I rather like. Inside the bag was an olive harvesting net, some twigs, an old child's shoe and a tiny, tiny kitten, the size of a hamster.

I was after some beers, but what is a man to do? Leave a kitten at the bins like some *malaka* did? Naaaaaa … that is not me, that is not Anne. What kind of person leaves a bunch of kittens in a plastic bag to die at some bins off a main road?

I did have one worry as I came back to the house with this bag of blind and deaf kittens … how many were there? We already had NINE. I had already seen pregnant stray females down in the bay with litters of five to eight kittens.

Anne opened the door to me holding beers in one hand and a yet to be defined number of kittens in a bag in the other - I had already seen a calico (orange, white, black) and a black and white kitten, but I had no idea just how many more were in there.

We carefully tipped the bag out onto a rug. Amongst the crudely cut olive netting were … THREE gorgeous kittens, tiny, just a few days old.

It was a Saturday evening, beer o'clock, and we had absolutely no idea what the hell to do to keep these gorgeous things alive. Anne put out a *'Bat Signal'* to all our friends in the area: vets, animal lovers, neighbours, animal organisations that we knew and within minutes the responses came flooding in. And continued to come in. It was amazing. Within an hour, from three different sets of people, we had formula to feed the kittens, bottles, advice on how to look after them, a cage to keep them in and offers of 24 hour help. I've never lived in what you might describe as a 'community' before, it felt so comforting. This was just another reason why I adore this place.

Chapter Twenty Nine: A Crazy End to 2020 - Lasers, a Serious Lack of Sleep and Kittens.

I never wanted kids, neither did Anne. What kind of world would we leave them? Humans don't deserve this Earth.

However I found myself in late 2020, in the middle of brain tumour treatment, as a father of three - THREE - tiny kittens. Our friends had told us that their chances of survival were not great, around 50/50, so it would be prudent to not give them names.

Their chances were slim due to their lack of a mother and due to their age, estimated at 4 days. Their eyes were shut, so they were blind. Their ears were closed, so they were deaf. They still had umbilical cords attached to them. They had been cruelly torn away from their mother and left to die. Who could do such a thing and abandon them to a slow and almost certain death?

We had taken on a huge challenge at the time we were least able to complete it. Local animal charities were overwhelmed with strays, but helped out with advice and tutorials as best they could.

But what could we do? Leave them? Not under our watch, no way. Yes, I was badly ill, yes, we would have to be back and forth to Athens for my treatment, yes, we would have to bottle feed them every 3 hours throughout the day and night, but this just brought out the utter stubbornness in us both. I really felt at the time that if the world wanted to chuck anything at me, anything at all, that my inherited stubbornness would take it as a challenge, a fun one at that, and stick two fingers up at it.

I didn't realise it at the time, but it was also the perfect distraction from all of the bad things going on around us. We just had to focus on waking up at the right time and keeping these little critters alive. We decided to raise them then look to put them up for adoption, as we already had nine cats (one above the indication of madness according to my Aunty Cathy) and three more would take us to twelve.

BEEP BEEP BEEP

BEEP BEEP BEEP

PRESS SNOOZE ON ALARM

BEEP BEEP BEEP

DRAG OUR SORRY ASSES OUT OF BED

PREPARE FORMULA AND FEED THREE HAMSTER SIZED KITTENS OF 120g EACH

WEIGH, NOTE WEIGHT IN JOURNAL, WIPE THEIR BUMS

PUT BACK IN CAGE

ANOTHER THREE HOURS OF SLEEP

… and repeat for weeks.

We had been taught to weigh the kittens after every meal to check for any sudden losses in weight, which would indicate a problem of some sort. I still have the chart monitoring this and it is a little sad to see, as across the top of the page are crudely named kittens: 'Calico, Black & White and Black & White Splodge' - we took the earlier advice and didn't name them.

Another lesson we were taught was that we had to imitate the mother, who would lick the kittens to stimulate them into going to the loo. It broke my heart to think that out there somewhere was a mother who should have been doing this, who had carried these three for months. Instead the job was being done by two rank amateurs - although not *literally* of course, wet cotton wool did the trick nicely.

But the good news, from the amount that they were eating (about a bottle of formula each kitten, each feed) and from the weigh-in chart, was that all three were putting on weight rapidly. We began to have just the slightest hope that they would make it.

Then one day, about a week after submitting all the necessary documentation, the insurance company gave the go ahead for my treatment. It was time to go to Athens. Our friends and tutors, Chris Spybey and Sue Lilley, had thankfully offered to look after the kittens while we were away. They had forgotten more than we will ever know on this subject and have raised absolutely loads of kittens by bottle while running their cat rescue shelter down at a local beach. The kittens were in the most capable hands they could hope for.

In very early November we once more made our way to Athens. It was still lockdown, so once again we had to have special documents from the hospital to say that we were traveling for medical reasons. The road up there is a wonderfully empty toll road, which means that it is very easy to be stopped by the police, but we had no issues.

The hospital told me to be in Athens for the next Monday and that the treatment would last until the Friday. Anne and I didn't want to stay in a hotel and instead found a nice 2 bedroom Airbnb apartment about an eight minute walk from the hospital, in a lovely suburb of Athens called Chalandri (Χαλάνδρι). It was quiet, overlooked lovely communal gardens (with a resident wild tortoise) where we could relax, cook and live as normal a life as possible, given I had no idea really how the treatment would affect me.

The treatment really was something else. I count myself incredibly lucky to be born when I was, for so many reasons, but this was just one more of them. If I were to be getting treatment for the tumour 10-15 years ago, I would have either had to have the awful operation I described in the previous chapter where they take off 25% of my skull for four months, or I could endure maybe 20-25 radiation sessions with the resulting sickness and loss of hair.

Unfortunately over the past five years I have seen the inside of too many hospitals and had too many consultations to remember. But one thing has been etched in my mind almost from the beginning: the advances being made in medicine - even in the last five years - astound me. They melt my brain, although I should point out in this instance, just metaphorically.

But I was having CyberKnife Treatment, a new non-invasive way of treating tumours. The patient lies back on a bed and what can be best described as a robotic arm moves around your head for the period of the session, firing radiation at the tumour from all angles. It is pre-programmed and rather than target the full tumour, it aims at one particular spot. In months of describing this process I have never been able to remember the exact words that the doctor used, but it was equivalent to the 'power source' of the tumour, the thing that is giving life to this invader in my cranium. Kill the energy, kill the tumour. All the time the laser has to miss vital parts of the brain and also vital organs which, given that the tumour was right behind my right eye, was particularly worrying. Even if successful (which is 90%-95% - odds I can happily live with) the tumour will never disappear. It is a visitor for life unfortunately. But what the doctors look for is signs that the tumour is dying ('necrosis') and also that it is effectively shutting up shop ('calcification').

All of this would take two days of preparation and three CyberKnife sessions, each lasting no longer than one hour. The best bit was that there were no side effects, although that is a point I will come back to later on.

But enough about that, let's get back to one of my favourite subjects … FOOD!

You remember up there I said we wanted an Airbnb to live a normal life, cook etc? I love cooking, but the most I 'cooked' in that time was a cup of tea and even that is stretching the definition of the word.

Why the hell should I? I was in Athens, I could have any food I wanted, and after all … I was an ill man, so who would dare argue with me? You've got to try and find some positives amongst a sea of negatives.

Yes, it was lockdown, but that turned out even better. We signed up to the Greek version of Deliveroo, efood, and the turnaround speeds were astounding, averaging about 30 minutes from online order to actual physical delivery. We'd buzz the delivery guy in, put a mask on as per the law, hand him a tip and take charge of our order as it had already been paid online. (Sorry if this is mansplaining to most of you, I'm just not used to it, having left the UK 11 years ago. Having Deliveroo in London in 2010 would have been *dangerous to our waistlines!*).

First night was grilled dumplings and dipping sauce, a quarter crispy duck and pancakes, crispy chilli beef, chicken satay and special fried rice. I forget what Anne had.

Day One was a nice easy introduction to the treatment. Security around the hospital was tough because of Covid, but I registered easily and all my insurance documents were perfectly in order.

I met a few doctors, including my main consultant, Olga, who has been right by my side throughout this whole process and has been worth her weight in gold. We went through the usual medical history, what prescription drugs I was taking, allergies etc.

Olga then explained what I could expect with the treatment, being a preparation day tomorrow, then a treatment with the CyberKnife for three days running. She said no juices like grapefruit or orange should be drunk and minimal alcohol. Having been trained in conditioning as part of negotiation tactics for work, I suggested that minimal would be maybe three beers?

She said 'more like two', which of course was my goal all along.

And that was it for the first day. I walked out, went 'home', had a nap and then got up.

Oh yeah, Indian, in case you were wondering, with the best Peshawari naan I have had in my life, it was like a cake!

I wish day two was as much fun. I would end up staggering out of the hospital, a complete, discombobulated mess.

I had read up a lot on what to expect from CyberKnife treatment and was unsure about this part. Posts on a few internet fora had got me a little worried.

First I met a consultant and he asked me the usual questions and then put a cannula in my right hand. Then back out to the waiting room. While I was waiting for this first consultant, I started sketching out these final few chapters of the book, as I waited about an hour. Now I had another wait, so I decided to do sketch out another chapter of pointers to stop me going off on tangents.

Ever tried writing with a cannula in your right hand? Not a chance, it hurts like hell (see earlier chapters).

I had my MRI scan, which was a walk in the park. Claustrophobia isn't a problem for me anymore, a nice 30 minute kip in a techno club and I was done. These would be the scans that they would be working off to see if any change was evident in the tumour over 6,9, 12 months etc.

Next I was told that I had to go for a CT scan. An MRI is where they place your full body in a fairly tight fitting dark tube. A CT scan is more like being pushed on a bed into a giant Polo mint, with only your head actually in the device. This is more like it!

The doctor explained that this stage had two aims. Firstly, to exactly identify the location of my tumour so that the CyberKnife system could be programmed to perform its work on me. The second aim was to make a mask for me. This would be very tight fitting, to within 1mm error of margin, and would be the thing I would wear during the CyberKnife treatment. It would be fixed to the table so I couldn't move, to make sure that the laser targeted the tumour and not an eye, for example.

The mask was made out of a flexible plastic sheet, kept warm in what looked like a sous-vide from a professional chef's kitchen. This kept the plastic pliable until it cooled down.

Before I had the CT scan, the doctor explained why I had been fitted with a cannula. It was to allow them to easily put intravenous contrasting agent into my bloodstream. It meant that the blood flowing through the brain showed up to a greater degree to the doctors/technicians monitoring my napper, allowing them to more accurately identify the tumour.

I am going to put a warning in now for the squeamish. If detailed medical procedures aren't your thing, or if highly personal issues aren't your thing, skip to the next cat paw. If a thoroughly embarrassing personal experience, where the joke is on me is your thing, please read on.

The doctor told me that the contrasting agent would make my blood feel very warm. He said it would start off warm, then get warmer, but not to worry because it stabilises and then very quickly subsides. Fair warning. No mention of my ass though. Nope, not a mention at all.

What a strange comment for me to make, you might think?

I was moved into the CT scanner and was told I couldn't move a centimetre. All fine.

'OK, agent going innnnnnn … NOW!'

Oh bloody **HELL! WHAT FRESH HELL IS THIS!? IT'S GETTING HOTTER! NO, IT'S GETTING WORSE AND I CAN'T EVEN MOVE OR SHOUT OR SCREAM! THIS IS LIKE A LETHAL INJECTION! IT'S SO FLIPPING HOT!**

It really was the worst medical experience ever. Well, at least for the next five minutes.

But, forewarned is forearmed, at least I knew what to expect. Or did I?

Remember my rather strange comment just a couple of paragraphs ago? Yeah, so they told me that my veins would have lava flowing through them - fine. They told me it would get worse and so it did. They also told me it would stabilise and it did. But no one, nobody, not a SOUL, warned me that my asshole would vaporise; turn into Mount Etna.

I struggled, strained, clenched, even prayed, I did absolutely all I could to prevent a 'Code Brown', but I was in agony and I needed a toilet very, very soon, as in, like, **NOW**.

A 'Code Brown' really wouldn't have been a good look in beige shorts, just a t-shirt, no change of clothes and an eight minute walk home.

Crisis was averted by a whisker, but it was close. Closer than close.

Worse was yet to come. While still struggling to contain myself, they decided it was time for the mask fitting. Again, I had been warned, but it was way worse than I understood it to be, and all just a minute after I had averted 'Bumhole Armageddon'.

A very large piece of hot, white meshed plastic was taken out of the 'sous vide' and placed over my face. Two people using sponges constantly moulded it to my face, as the fit had to be exact.

It felt like waterboarding. My sinuses have never been good and I couldn't breathe, I couldn't move due to the targeting and I feared another 'Code Brown' coming on.

It has horrible, but after an epic toilet break, that was Stage One done.

I left the hospital in a bewildered state, a state of shock, not really sure what just happened.

… But at least I didn't brown my tweeds.

I went home and attempted to explain it all to Anne. In what I guess was a bit of a coping mechanism throughout these months I would just joke about the whole thing and now I had one more story. I called the process 'Tumour Humour'.

Oh, and in case you were wondering, 2 x XL Dominos pizzas, 2 x chicken strippers, extra BBQ sauce.

Day three was the start of CyberKnife treatment, highly targeted radiation at the base, the 'power source' of the tumour. I was daunted, but the success rates were very good and the chances of side effects were slim.

I shouldn't have worried. I went down to the -5 Level basement of this iceberg of a hospital and met the lovely doctor who would be my guide through the next three days. She was so relaxed, fun, answered any questions in really easy to understand soundbites - just precisely what you would wish for in this situation.

Just before my treatment was due to start she asked if I had any further questions. As a matter of fact, I did!

'Can you take a few photos of me on my iPad please so I can show everyone this crazy machine?'

'Of course'

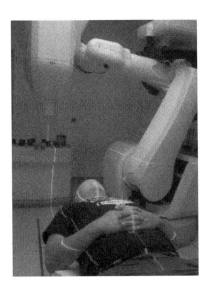

The CyberKnife

The world's worst Dr Evil Impression

As she handed me back the iPad she said 'Guy, that final pose, with your little finger hanging out of the side of your mouth, what was all that about please?'

'That's Dr Evil from the film Austin Powers!'

Blank stare

'You know, with Mike Myers in, and Dr Evil is going to use a massive LAAAAYYYYZEEERRRR to hold the world to ransom and he puts his finger in his mouth like that? I'm about to be LAAAAYYYYZEEERRRR-ed too!'

Yet another blank stare

We began the treatment. I lay down and my mask was placed over me and fastened in four places to the bed. I couldn't move my head, but didn't feel restricted or uncomfortable in any way.

Directly above my head were pictures of rainforests and exotic birds and there was chill-out music on.

I lay there doing some basic estimation and arithmetic and worked out that the lovely, amazingly educated and trained Doctor I had been boring ten minutes previously probably hadn't even been born when the Austin Powers film came out, a film that we watched back to back all night in our grotty student house in Birmingham. This is what it is like to get old. The kids smile and nod, they don't have any idea what oldie is on about.

How did I get so old so quickly?

Before I knew it, I had fallen asleep and was snoring so loud it woke me up with what should have been a jolt - except I was wearing my mask, which was fastened to the table which stopped any movement. I then noticed that I was being seriously eyed up by this robot arm. It was a few inches from my face, firing off red lasers at the enemy within. I then watched it move around and attack the other side, then from above and then I think I fell asleep again.

The whole 'ordeal' lasted 57 minutes and then I was done for the day.

Days Four and Five were the same routine, yet slightly shorter sessions, of around 40 minutes each. That meant that I had received the highest dosage of radiation recommended for anyone to have in a week.

After the second CyberKnife session on Day Four I felt incredibly tired so I came home and slept for a fair chunk of the afternoon. I woke up to the news that they had developed an effective vaccine for Covid!

What a game changer! Or so it seemed at the time. Like I said, the medical fraternity never fail to astound me. It was only a month or two ago that we were being told that they might never find a vaccine and now they had one with very high efficacy rates!

What a week!

1. CyberKnife on my tumour!

2. Covid vaccine announced! (With, we would later hear, several more to come).

3. Trump lost! Not that he accepted it, but I decided then and there to maybe take 2022 off, stock up on popcorn and network subscriptions and watch every minute of him and his disgusting family on trial. Now that's what I call entertainment!

I had asked for my final CyberKnife treatment to be early on the Friday morning so we could get home as soon as possible, as I missed the place and the animals so much. The hospital couldn't have been more accommodating and I was walking out of the door, treatment completed, before 9am!

Anne had been packing the car and cleaning up the flat since I left that morning, so we were good to go as soon as I got back and were back on our mountain at 1pm that day. I drove the first 3 hours until I got tired, Anne did the last hour. 10-15 years ago, the possibility of driving after treatment would have been unheard of. To the medical community: I salute you!

The cats gave us a great welcome, as did Floyd when we picked her up from Eirini's. But one thing was missing: the kittens. We went down to Chris and Sue's house to find them completely changed, even in the space of a week. There were eating solids, using the litter tray, almost even behaving themselves.

By way of thanks we had brought down what might be a contender for Greece's longest takeaway delivery, clocking in at four hours. Chris and Sue love Indian food and the nearest Indian to us at the time was in Athens.

If you are thinking that we ordered a whole load for them on Day Two of Athens and kept it in the fridge, don't be silly. Why waste an opportunity to get another lovely takeaway? So that is what we had another great Indian the night before we left, adding an extra special order on for a pair of extra special people. I must admit I was tempted to steal a little bit of that amazing Peshawari naan that was like cake, but I resisted the temptation.

Back at home we still kept the kittens caged at night as they were still too small to be let out the whole time, but we let them out all the time that we were around, let them out on the terrace to wander around.

What had seemed like something we just HAD to do - who could leave four day old kittens by a bin to die? - had now turned into a very nice diversion from the harsh realities of life. Lockdown was harder this second time. I had a brain tumour. Oh, yes, and I forgot to mention, Anne and I were both made redundant in June - the reason for starting this book. Anne had worked for her company - a lovely company - but one taken over by a giant corporation that was far less appreciative of its staff - for over ten years. The first she heard of the news was an email. No phone call, nothing. Ten years. It was a zero hours contract too, so not a penny was due in redundancy payment. Hello furlough.

Friends and neighbours rallied round and took the kittens for weekends which were just golden breaks. We were shattered and it was such a boost.

We would hand the cage over to our lovely friends, have a nice sleep in, long breakfast, then in the evening, around 5pm, call my mate Vasilis and order spit roast lamb, spit roast pork with crackling, chips, rice, salads, and drink vodka in bed whilst eating our feast and watching the latest boxset or a film on the TV at the end of our bed.

By the Monday we would want them back so much, but those breaks made the world of difference to us.

Over the ten years we had spent together, 99% of the time just us and the animals, Anne and I had almost become telepathic.

Me: 'I know there is no way you are putting these three up for adoption and neither am I'.

Anne: 'No chance'

I challenge anybody to rescue three hamster sized kittens, go through all the heartache and irregular hours of bottle feeding, worry about whether they will survive and then say 'OK, let's find a new home for them shall we?'

No, our rather gargantuan food and vaccination and vet bills are just going to have to rise by 33%. (I should add that the vets, our friends Kostas and Melina are not expensive at all, but have you seen how much 12 cats can eat!?).

Me: 'Right, they are well over a kilo, they are past the worst - we need to name them'.

We had a calico (orange, white and black) and two black and white kittens.

There are certain rules in the cat world when it comes to cat characteristics that hold 90% of the time. Firstly, trying to ascertain the sex of a kitten at this young age is very difficult. Secondly, the colour gives away a lot. A ginger is almost always going to be a Tom Cat, a male. A Tortie is almost always going to be female and also a handful, hence the expression 'Troublesome Torties', although our beloved Franklin was anything but troublesome. White cats are almost always deaf and here in Greece, if they are pets, you should always consider having much of their outer ear removed as they will often contract cancer from the sun on pale skin. Calicos are almost always female.

Again, I stress, none of these rules are hard and fast, but they mostly hold.

We had two black and white kittens that we assumed to be boys and a calico that we assumed to be a girl.

To the boys:

1. The most playful and fun - although they all could lay claim to that - was a black and white one with a black smudge near his nose. Many years ago when we lived in London, Anne and I went on a long walk through Highgate Woods and ended up in a pub called The Wrestlers, where the most amazing dog was lying in front of the fire. He was so friendly and we got chatting to the owner and she said he was called 'Woodstock'. We loved the name and stuck it in the back of our minds for safekeeping. Not only the legendary festival (legendary only if you weren't there and could watch it later on DVD from the comfort of your sofa with a toilet nearby, as they didn't have any toilets for half a million people), but also a Snoopy character. Woodstock it is. Done. Meet Woodstock everybody:

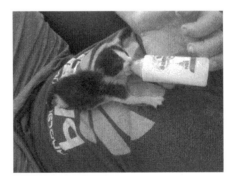

2. For ages I had wanted an animal named after another one of my absolute heroes. Now was my time. This guy had a voice of velvet, his backing band was so tight (Booker T and the MGs, later recording 'Green Onions', a childhood favourite from my dad). On 10th December 1967, a week after recording one of my favourite songs in

the world, and not long after playing the famous Monterey Pop Festival, where Jimi Hendrix first became known to many people, he and his band got on a plane that never made its destination, crashing into Lake Wisconsin, killing almost all aboard.

I had already named Oswald, Ozzy, after Ozzy Osbourne, who only avoided dying because he had a hangover and didn't get into the light aircraft that his genius guitar player, Randy Rhoads, died in when the plane buzzed the bus, a wing caught the side and it crashed, killing all aboard.

So allow me to introduce Otis, the second of our three new additions. The song Otis recorded a week before his untimely death at just 26, which posthumously became his only number one in 1968 was one of the best ever recorded, (Sittin' on) The Dock of the Bay. Just think of what this amazing man could have achieved were his life not cut so cruelly short, just like Randy Rhoads.

MUSICIANS I LOVE - PLEASE, DO NOT GET INTO PLANES!

3. This leaves us with our only female, a calico who was so mischievous and fun. Many calicos here are mostly white, with the orange and black marking a secondary feature, but not this one.

I had been a bit pushy naming the kittens, although Woodstock was a joint choice. I said to Anne that this was hers, but make it cool.

We went through all of her favourite punk icons, 80s musicians with their terrible drum sounds (Anne disputes this, she is wrong unfortunately), you name it. Then Anne put on one of her favourite records. It was by 'The Toy Dolls', a punk band from her home town of Sunderland. Before I met her, I had only seen their cover of 'Nellie the Elephant' on Top of the Pops, which, yes, was terrible, but how many bands have released terrible cover singles that 'defined' them to most people, yet left behind a really good body of work? A favourite band of mine once was The Wonderstuff. Everybody says to me 'I hate Size of a Cow and Dizzy'. Yeah? So do I - but listen to those two first albums and you will hear a different band.

The Toy Dolls have had an amazing career, still playing still touring, until Covid ruined the most effective way for musicians to earn a crust.

While in lockdown, the singer from the Toy Dolls, Michael Algar (known as 'Olga') devised a very clever way to earn some money while he couldn't tour - he did online guitar lessons, and that boy sure plays a mean geee-tar. Anne signed up for them, but with all the craziness she is still yet to start them.

Anne suggested Olga as a name - her hero, and also the name of my guardian angel at the hospital and it just seemed right ... until you imagined shouting the name 'Olga' out from the front door.

Anne: 'OK, I agree - what about Nellie?'

Done. Meet Nellie ...

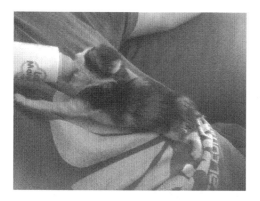

It was time to get them to the vet. We always follow the same procedure - as soon as we can get them chipped and vaccinated we do it, as soon as we can get them neutered we can, much as I hate the whole process, but it is the right thing to do.

Kostas is our fantastic local vet whom we have known for years. Even when he was asked about the sex of the kittens at such a young age, he wasn't 100% sure, but he said we had three girls.

HANG ON? Only yesterday we had TWO boys and a girl!?

He chipped, vaccinated and neutered each of our three new females and we went back home a different family, Otis now being Oti and we kept the name Woodstock

Our cat flap means that anyone can get out - just in case a stray somehow follows one of ours immediately - but that only those that are chipped and logged in the cat flap system are allowed out.

The technology for animals is amazing now and many years ago when our cats started first roaming for days and weeks Anne and I thought we had a killer product. We thought about strapping a small GPS onto a cat - or an implant - that could allow an owner to locate their cat at any time. We decided to call it *The Cat-Nav*, but research showed we had been beaten to it.

But I digress.

Our usual route is to not force new kittens into anything, just to let them find their way. Some are immediate and just jump out into this new world of hundreds of acres of adventure - not all ours I might add. Others take their time, watch their friends … and then do nothing … The longest it has taken is 3 weeks, the shortest … maybe one minute?

Within weeks they were out patrolling our fields, olive groves, and all the surrounding land. We would have voles, rats and cicadas as presents, the occasional snake, often alive - thanks for all those sleepless nights you lot!

L-R: Oti, Woodstock and Nellie.

As previously noted during my treatment in Athens, late 2020 saw Greece in lockdown again for the second time. There were a raft of restrictions, far tougher than many countries, many that didn't affect me, but the ones that did were:

1. You had to either get an SMS message or fill out a form to allow you to leave the house.

2. You had to always carry with you both your passport and your residency permit.

3. There was an evening curfew of 10pm.

4. You could only exercise from your house, so for example I couldn't do my usual and drive down to a beach and walk Floyd along it.

5. There were fines of €150 for breaking the rules. My friend broke the curfew by accident and showed me his fine. I heard of a family who went swimming in the sea (also not allowed). 4 x €150 = one very expensive family swim.

6. Cafés, tavernas and bars were all shut, but takeaways were allowed.

7. No fishing from the land. Eh? A bloke standing on a rock hundreds of metres from others can't dip a line in?

The second Greek lockdown started in Autumn 2021, whereas the previous one in 2020 started in March. Winter was over for the first one, the lovely weather had started, the amazing wild flowers were about and it was a bit of a novelty.

But this second lockdown was all through winter, not the worst winter we had seen here, but still. We had a new irritant, a constant irritant, one that affected our lives not just daily, but hourly as I will explain later.

That said, we really need to put this into perspective. Previous generations sat in trenches, 'went over the top', endured bombardment and gas. Their parents/families endured the Blitz.

We sat on our sofas eating food that was delivered to our door and watched Netflix. Should we complain?

But yes, the youngest generation, the ones that were leaving school with messed up A-Level results, maybe no university place and no option to go travelling had every right to complain.

2020 ended in a strange old way. Anne and I were in bed by 8pm, without a huge amount to celebrate.

The fishing village below us, Agios Nikolaos, put on their NYE fireworks, but two hours early, due to the curfew.

That said, there was lot to be happy about:

1. My treatment was over and we waited for the results.

2. A vaccine to Covid had been found.

3. The four times bankrupt, racist, lying, orange, 45th President was on his way out.

Chapter Thirty: 2021 - Goodbye, Yieasas, Kalinixta, I'm Outta Here.

I started the year with a big headache, something that probably wasn't too unusual to many around the world. But I had been in bed, sober at 8pm.

Once again, every day for what would become four to five months, I got headaches and nothing I took would relieve the pain. Every. Day. For. Four. To. Five. Months.

Ever had back pain? Toothache? I've been pretty lucky to not need immediate treatment and be in constant pain every hour of the day. I once accidentally cut my eye on the sharp end of a yucca leaf, which I really wouldn't recommend. One side of my face swelled up to a horrible size, my eye completely closed up, and it was total, total, pain.

I drank a bottle wine to get rid of the pain. Nothing. Anne went to bed and I tried to sleep, but the pain was too much. At about 2am, I drank another bottle of wine, but it too did nothing. I tried to sleep again, but couldn't sleep due to the pain.

At about 4am Anne was woken by a dull thudding sound - it was me kicking the wall. I was going so crazy that I wanted a different kind of pain to take over from the one in my eye. It was driving me mad, just like these constant headaches starting in January 2021 would. Thankfully we lived 5 minutes' drive away from Moorfields Eye Hospital and they sorted me out straight away - what a relief!

Gardening seems to me to be a very hazardous pastime. I remember back in the Gordon Brown government, so pre-2010, one of the most distinguished British scientists, Professor David Nutt, was engaged to carry out an in-depth study on the relative harms caused by drugs and also other activities. Predictably, heroin and crack - both Class A and highly illegal - came out top. But other drugs, completely legal, were in the top five too: alcohol and tobacco. Furthermore, Professor Nutt came to the conclusion that ecstasy, the scourge of the tabloid newspapers from about 1988-1995, was safer to take than going horse riding. I'd say gardening way more dangerous than both ecstasy *and* horse riding - a lethal pastime.

Just as an aside, the government didn't like what a top scientist they had chosen had to say on the subject because it didn't suit their narrative. How can we have some of the most harmful drugs legal - and producing billions of pounds in revenue, while putting people in prison for marijuana possession? - so what did they do? They terminated his employment, dumped him. This was a godsend to the puerile and childish tabloid media - whom I despise, but with this one I am with them. It is a childish headline writer's dream, an open goal of a headline: '*Nutt Sacked*'. Brilliant.

Back to the headaches. Nothing would cure them. They came almost all day, every day. There was no mistaking them.

My amazing consultant who treated me for the brain tumour, Olga, would respond almost immediately with a new prescription, another attempt to dull the pain. Imagine four or five months of constant pain, absolutely no respite - it is enough to drive you crazy.

Prescription four, my fourth changed prescription came and went - no use, it just couldn't shift the pain. I woke up one Saturday morning with yet another headache and Anne said 'I'm not having this anymore'. What came next was a perfect example of the kind of medical service you get here when you need it most, when you are crying out for help.

Anne emailed Olga. Olga would have been well within her rights to ignore the mail because it was the weekend, but she came back in 10 minutes with another drug suggestion, with the warning that if these didn't work we had no other option but an OxyContin style drug - you'll have heard of it by its more common slang name: 'Hillbilly Heroin'.

Anne then Facebooked Dr Sofia and asked if there was any way she could provide an emergency prescription. She replied straight away and she authorised the Pharmacy to give Anne the drug for me, with prescription to follow in normal office hours on Monday.

Then Anne messaged Konstantina, a friend of ours at the pharmacy, to ask if they had this particular drug. 'Yes, come right down'.

Anne went and collected this drug, something called Arcoxia and within an hour of Anne first contacting Olga in Athens I had the drug in my hand and took it. The headache was gone within 10 minutes.

It is impossible to put a price on service and help like that when you are going crazy with pain, but I love you all.

Olga wasn't convinced that the headaches were caused by the laser treatment, but I was in no doubt. It couldn't have been another tumour as I had had so many MRIs that it would have showed up. Oh, what *did* show up in the MRI was the fact that I have three herniated discs at the top of my spine that could have been there for years or decades. That might just explain why I can't even turn around enough to reverse a car. I believe it was there since birth, as I was a forceps birth, a very difficult one at that, and have had back and neck problems ever since. It took 46 years for it to be even discovered by doctors, of course because they weren't looking for it, but I believe I have had this for my whole life and just didn't know.

Having a herniated disc at the top of my neck as I had just found out, explained *everything*. That's one to sort after we've relaxed for a few years!

What was also less than encouraging was that Olga said that the radiation will be doing its thing inside my head for the next 18 months. 18 months more of this? Shoot me now.

In the background on our lovely tranquil mountain, some unexpected activity was occurring. We had been here nine years and very little building had been done. A half-finished house behind us was finished and a 90% finished house behind that was finished. We also had a swimming pool built that caused noise.

My next words should be taken in that context. We ourselves have had building work, so I am completely aware this is being written from a small hill of hypocrisy.

Many of my friends are builders, they deserve to earn a living and I support that. It is money that goes into the local economy and is one of really only three industries here: Building, Tourism and Olives.

But how about this for irony? We bought the plot of land next to us to stop someone from building there in 2019. Nothing new, absolutely nothing new, had been built in the entire nine years we have lived here. Yet in 2020, in the middle of a pandemic, a year after we bought some land to stop building we current have TWELVE houses being built with more rumoured to come.

For each house I would estimate about 4 weeks of this awful digging, constantly from 8am-4pm, Monday to Saturday inclusive, not even stopping for a lunch break. If the builders are of the non- law abiding types, they will often work until 8pm, although the record here is 11pm. Oh yes, they quite often like to work on Sundays as well.

Legal hours for noisy building vary throughout the year, but now they are 8am-3:30pm Monday to Saturday. Some weeks we didn't even get a day off. This went on for eighteen months, in fact it is still going on as I type.

We were not able to siesta, go to bed early, swim, use the garden or walk the dog quietly without the ear splitting noise coming from several sites.

February 2021: I *HATE* DIY. Hate it, hate it, hate it. I need to be in the right mood to even contemplate it. If I am in the right mood I say to Anne 'make a list and make it quick, I'll get it done'.

It was February, one of only two months I don't like here, together with August, there was driving rain, 80km/h winds and the door of the chicken coop - *Cluckingham Palace* - was hanging off its hinges. The job couldn't wait. I ignored the usual rule of bringing your entire tool box and equipment to the job as it will *always* save you time (a fine rule, to always be obeyed), and instead took a fistful of screws and nails in my left hand and my Bosch drill in the right.

I started to walk down the steep stone steps, in the driving rain and howling wind and then slipped …

I fell 3 metres and because I had nails and screws in my hand I couldn't use my hands to protect me as usual. The full impact was taken with my right cheekbone smashing on a rock, my knees were hurting badly, as were my wrists. I was a bloody, bruised mess.

I was completely dazed and shocked to a level I had never experience before. I had been in motorway pile ups with 30+ cars, I had come off a scooter and skidded across tough Camden tarmac. Nothing had come close to this.

As the area I fell into was the natural drainage point for this whole side of the mountain, I was in a swamp. I screamed 'HELP ME!', but no one came. I couldn't get up as I hurt so much, I couldn't get up as no one would have been able to in that swamp.

Another cry for 'HELP!'

Anne was working in the polytunnel and couldn't hear, but luckily a friend, Abi, who was house sitting for a neighbour heard me and came to help, by which time Anne had also heard me. They helped me, bruised and battered, back home for a bath with a few vodkas to calm the pain.

I should have had broken bones - certainly a cheekbone, probably an arm and maybe a leg - the fall was that bad. Instead I had a large collection of cuts and bruises and a very, very bruised and cut right cheekbone.

Why was that a problem? My brain tumour sat immediately behind my right eye, behind the right cheekbone that took the full impact. The tumour was so close to the eye that the eye would have been the tumour's first 'victim'. I emailed my specialist, Olga, again on a weekend, and she said I had to have another MRI.

I booked it for the next week, got in, slept for another 30 minutes of techno wearing a storm trooper's mask (*'made by my Aunt, dontchyaknow'*) and came out fine.

The technician asked if I was OK, and I just repeated my usual 'joke': 'Yeah, all fine, used to go to techno clubs in Birmingham in 1994 like that. The drugs were way better then though'. I think he was bored of that one by this stage.

I got that appointment almost immediately, in fact they offered me a few days earlier, but I was booked up. €120, results the next day. It would have been just €20 if I had a prescription, which I couldn't sort in time.

I gave the results to The Amazing Dr Sofia (can I stop putting 'the amazing' prefix on yet? No, not yet) and also to Olga, my consultant in Athens.

What happened next was wonderful. Olga told me that even in this early time after treatment, the MRI clearly showed promising signs of necrosis i.e. deterioration in the tumour. I wasn't even meant to see if it had worked for 6 months after the treatment.

I just broke down and cried and cried and cried.

Chapter Thirty-One: 'It's All Over Now For Me and EU'

On 31st January 2021 the UK officially left the EU, an organisation it had been part of since 1975, the year after my birth. As I mentioned before, as bad luck and poor timing would have it, Anne and I were in Sunderland that very day. Sunderland was one of the earlier regions to declare and was the first real sign that things were not going to plan for the Remain campaign, with 61.3% of voters voting to Leave.

It was poignant watching a few people celebrate in the pub, when I think time will show that it will be a turning point in that fine city's economic prospects; a city that has had more than its 'fair' share of economic problems. The last two economic crises were for reasons largely beyond their control. This one they had voted for and were proud of it. It was one of the biggest Leave majorities in the country.

It also left Anne and I and many other Brits out here in a state of stasis. We had Greek residency cards, but these expired on 1st January 2021. These had to be replaced with new biometric cards by 30th June 2021, for which you needed to prove that you were someone who benefited from the Withdrawal Agreement. Essentially you had to prove that you were resident in Greece before 31st December 2020, which is why you needed to keep your old, buff or blue, expired, residency card.

Many Brits I know that either lived here full time or planning to retire here didn't get their residency cards. I cannot get my head around why, but there are some possible explanations:

1. Uncertainty over the rules?

2. They didn't think they needed it? I heard a story of an English lady who came over in the 1980s, married a Greek man, worked, paid taxes, spoke the language fluently, raised two children and put them through university. She was as integrated as could be. But she was still a British citizen and needed a residency card.

3. Sadly, yes, I have heard the old 'they need us more than we need them' argument a few times too. 'They' honestly don't; they really don't. There were others that didn't realise that Freedom of Movement was a two-way thing, that if *we* stopped EU citizens coming into the UK to live and work, *they* could also stop *us* living and working in their EU countries. The lack of basic understanding from some parties - although by no means all - was equal parts staggering and depressing.

4. The 'Head in the Sand'. I also know of people scared to go through the process, who stuck their head in the sand, just hoping that it would just go away.

Technically everyone needed these biometric cards, Greeks included. But there was only one nationality queueing up at the Police Station - us Brits.

Why? Many people even now haven't heard of the 90/180 rule. This is something that applies to every Third Country National (TCN), i.e. anyone who is a citizen of any country - be it Japan or the US or, yes, the UK - that is not in the EU.

Part of the Freedom of Movement rules that made things so easy for Brits to travel, live and work in the EU was that we had the right to live and work in any other EU country for as long as we liked, as long as we registered. Now the UK was outside the EU, those benefits - and I do think they were benefits - no longer apply. UK citizens are treated the same as any other person from any other country around the world.

That meant the 90/180 rule. Put simply, as a non-EU citizen or resident, you are allowed to spend just 90 days in the Schengen Zone in any 180 day period. You could come out to Greece and stay for just under three months and then you would have to leave. Failure to do so attracts some fairly heavy fines and repeated breaches could involve jail time.

Say, for example, you wanted to spend a romantic weekend in Paris, then come down to your holiday home for a three month stay. You'd be breaching the 90/180 rule, as France is also in the Schengen Zone and the rule covers the overall zone, not just the individual countries within it.

Or, as often happens here, you own a holiday home and want to do what you have done for years, get some sun on the first flight in April, returning in September. That is six months, so again, against the rule.

The Brits therefore were the only ones getting biometric cards because everyone else from the EU could just walk in and stay as long as they liked, just as we once could.

The one phrase that I have seen so many times that winds me up the most is around what rules the UK applies to EU citizens in the same respect. The UK has been more relaxed, generous, and has said that while the total number of days in a year that EU citizens can stay is 180 - the same as the EU - the UK allows those 180 days to be taken in one go, which makes things far easier. The 90/180 rule does not apply.

I've heard and read people saying 'We let them take their 180 days in one go, and yet we have the 90/180 day rule - they are punishing us for trying to Leave'. This ignores the fact that the EU has had this 90/180 policy for many, many years. It applies to every single non-EU country on the planet, not just the UK. Lastly, which nation voted in favour of this arrangement? Yes, you guessed it, the UK.

I've also heard the 'why can't they make an exception for us, we were part of the EU for ages, think of all that money we gave them'. I'll leave that with no further comment.

Under the terms of the Withdrawal Agreement, we could get 'Permanent Residency', which in reality was a ten year visa, so I would argue was a significant distance from my understanding of the definition of 'permanent'. We had to collate the usual documents, plus 5 years of tax returns for us both, new photos etc and go the Police Station in Kalamata.

As we walked in past a Police officer with a sub-machine gun my stomach started churning, remembering the difficulties we all had last time. But this was a different set up, a different station and the Police officer who processed our application could not have been more friendly or helpful.

You effectively have to prove that you have the means to live in Greece (house deeds, rental agreement etc), the money to do so (salary slip, savings accounts etc) and the ability to not be a burden on the Greek health system (private health insurance). It is not clear yet if we have to prove this again in ten years or we get a straight swap. If the former, it is a little worrying - think how your own health and finances have changed in ten years.

We were done in 10 minutes, all we had to do was come back a week later, have our fingerprints taken and then pick the finished card up a week after that. The admin fee was €16. As a process it couldn't have been better, friendlier or easier. It is so sad to see that the Settled Status scheme in the UK seems to be the opposite of this.

We also had to change our driving licences (€16 fee) and that was equally painless.

Buuuuut ... the bureaucracy wasn't over yet, and I should add that this bureaucracy wasn't all Greek - most of it was due to a UK decision.

We needed our Covid jab. For this you needed your AMKA number (Social Security). We didn't have ours as you only become eligible for them after ten years of residency, or if you work here. You couldn't go private either. Many people were caught in the same trap, so the government set up a temporary AMKA scheme, 'PAMKA'. But this was somewhat chaotic and we could see the tourist season looming and wanted to be jabbed. It took us about 6 weeks to get an appointment.

I can understand that the government needed to get a system put into place to track who had had the jab, when, what does (in case of a faulty batch) etc.

AstraZeneca was the only available vaccine here, so we had that. The first jab was fine, I went for a short kip and awoke 17 hours later. Both of us were fine on the second jab too.

Now Bill Gates could track us and see just how boring we both are!

In previous chapters I have listed the very few things I miss about the UK, but one thing was top of the list: Asian food. Boy, I missed it. Sure, I could cook it and have spent many a fun afternoon cooking up a curry crescent of many different dishes, but I guess the lazy part of me just mourned for the days when you could ring someone up and within 45 minutes get an amazing array of different dishes without really lifting a finger.

One of the very best things about 2021 was the opening of MYLO Indian Restaurant down in the bay.

Many people (almost all tourists) on local fora were saying that an Indian restaurant had no place in a Greek village. I assume they eat English food 100% of the time, three meals a day, seven days a week? Variety is the spice of life and I was so excited. I decided to be the first ever customer, inspired by the fans of Apple products who camped out on the street overnight to be the first to buy the latest iPhone.

We turned up for the first table on the first day of opening to see a family leaving, having had their meal. What!? OK, so I was the second person to ever eat there, but I am sure in time, when memories fade, I can change, embellish the narrative to make me the first.

It was amazing and I notice that on their TripAdvisor post, there are three photos: two of food, one of me, so I am now a brand ambassador!

Chapter Thirty-Two: 'This is The End … Beautiful Friend, The End'.

Lockdown ended. The vaccination rollout was good, although many countries had a greater take-up. There is still some scepticism here.

I can't imagine a job as difficult as being in a government of a country where Covid is on the rise, but where 20% of the economy depends upon tourism. It is a lose/lose situation. Keep Covid restrictions in place and the economy tanks, local businesses fold. At the other end of the spectrum, let a load of people from other parts of Greece like Athens, with higher infection rates, plus people from all around the world and Covid will spread faster, infections will rise and the death toll will mount. It is a thankless task and not one I would want to perform.

For what it's worth, I think they have found a decent balance this year in a really tough environment.

I am old enough to remember when traveling was fun. These days it just seems to be ever changing regulations, testing, traffic light systems, testing on landing, testing when you return. But never underestimate the desire of people to see the sun and to come to Greece. Our part of The Mani was open for business and ready to welcome visitors to enjoy and spend money in the local economy.

OK, well, after one false start (a 'false start' trying to stop writing? Hmmmm …) this really is it. The End … Beautiful Friends … The End. Thank you for making it this far.

P.S. One final thing: I went to Messini this week for an MRI scan. This was to see if the treatment in Athens had worked and whether this unwanted, unwelcome squatter in my brain was still alive and growing.

The results took two days and my consultant in Athens got the results at the same time. My phone rang, it was Olga, my consultant.

'*Guy, these are telio*' ('perfect'). The tumour had shrunk a lot and she said she thought it was dead. I won't lie, there were more tears involved. The radiation will be with me working on what is left of the tumour for another year or so too.

I had won the biggest battle of my life without really lifting a finger, just having the best team one could wish for on my side.

Appendix - 'The Life of Briam' - My Interpretations of Classic Greek Recipes

Cooking and eating food are a passion for me and I adore Greek food. We eat out regularly at the many tavernas down in the bay.

Certain food, such as Thai, or Anne's favourite, Cadbury's Creme Eggs, cannot be found anywhere nearby and so I do my best to recreate them at home. Most ingredients are commonly available, and those that aren't, such as coriander, I grow.

I'd say my success rate is pretty acceptable, but when it goes wrong it can go horribly, sometimes comically, wrong. Take the Creme Eggs. Make the filling, one white, one yellow, scrunch up a teaspoon of yellow filling into an outer layer of white filling in the palm of your hand. Then place a souvlaki stick in the 'egg' and dip it in melted chocolate. Let the 'Creme Egg' solidify using half a raw potato as a base for the souvlaki stick. Simple, eh?

Well, perhaps for some. The photo on the left is how they should look. The photo on the right is my effort.

Whenever I have a great dish at a local tavern, I do my best to recreate it at home, starting with some online recipes and adding bits and pieces as I go along.

Over the years these recipes have been refined and so I am fairly confident that if you follow them you will get a truly authentic- tasting Greek dish. That said, I would never show these to a Greek friend as they would probably laugh whilst pointing out error after error.

In my experience, Greek cooking does not have to be precise, unlike other forms of cooking, or baking. As such, ingredients in the recipes are not normally given in exact stated weights, more a rough description of what is needed.

Each recipe feeds two, but I usually make double and freeze the rest, or, more usually, eat it the next day. *Kali orexi!*

'The Life of Briam': **My Interpretations of Classic Greek Recipes**

1. Kleftiko

Of all the Greek dishes, this is my favourite. As a winter warmer it is up there with a Sunday roast with all the trimmings, but is way easier to cook. Essentially it is tender, slow cooked marinated meat with vegetables that have been at the bottom of the greaseproof parcel that holds this dish together, cooking in the meat juices, olive oil, herbs and other goodies. On the top is a load of melted cheese because … well, why not?

It's a knockout meal. I usually make double this amount, enough for four kleftika, and freeze two. They reheat brilliantly and they are also a great dish to part cook and just reheat with half an hour of notice and minimal extra effort perhaps if you are having guests around.

I have used beef in the ingredients, but really, it doesn't matter what meat you use, it will all come out lovely and tender. Lamb is traditional, beef and pork is very common in my village and if you have any offcuts of all the meats then just mix and match! The oregano and thyme used when I make kleftika is taken from our field, where huge bushes grow wild.

Ingredients:

500g beef (or the same amount of pork, lamb, or two chicken fillets)
3 large potatoes
2 normal sized carrots
1 pepper
1 courgette
1 large clove garlic (or more if that is your thing)
1 large tomato
1 large red onion
Cheese (ideally Feta, Cheddar or Kasseri - but not blue cheese)
Olive oil
Oregano, thyme (dried or fresh)
Red wine vinegar

Lemon juice
Seasoning
Greaseproof paper

Total Preparation Time: 30 minutes

Total Cooking Time: 90 minutes

Method:

1. Slice the meat into thin strips, about 1cm thick. Put into a bowl, add a good glug of olive oil to cover everything, a nice splash of lemon juice (equivalent to 3 squeezed lemons or more if you like) and some red wine vinegar. Cover the meat in the oregano and the thyme and the crushed garlic and give everything a good season with salt and pepper and a stir.

Either leave to marinate and refrigerate in the bowl, or a nice time-saving trick is to put it in a freezer bag to save you having to keep turning the meat.

As a minimum, this should marinate for 1-2 hours. Overnight is even better.

2. Boil a kettle and turn on the oven to 180 degrees if fan (200 degrees if not).

3. Peel the potatoes and cut them into finger sized shapes. Chop the courgettes into slices, peel and chop the carrots.

4. Add the potatoes to a large saucepan (bigger than is needed for just them), add boiling water and salt, boil on full heat for 8 minutes.

5. In the meantime, slice the red onion, pepper and the tomatoes and place on a plate.

6. Once the potatoes have boiled for 8 minutes, add the chopped courgette and carrots. Set another alarm for 6 minutes.

7. While you are waiting for that, prepare your casing. Each kleftiko is held together by greaseproof paper when cooking. Allow 40cm from a standard roll of greaseproof paper per kleftiko.

8. Once the alarm goes, drain the veg and allow them to cool for a few minutes. The vegetables should be nicely cooked, not hard.

You can now start to assemble your kleftika. I like the production line style, especially when making four and kleftika are made in layers.

On each piece of paper, place a layer of the boiled vegetables (potato, carrot, courgette).

Then add the meat.

Then add the raw tomato and red onion.

9. Close up each parcel by bringing the long edges together and rolling them up together, then scrunch up each end.

10. Put on a baking tray in the oven for an hour. Once this hour is over and you are pre-preparing food for eating later, perhaps when friends arrive, that is you done - go and relax.

11. If you are eating straight away, chop up the cheese to go in. I tend to put a few pieces the size of a small matchbox in each kleftiko, so unroll each of them, add the cheese and then set an alarm for a further 30 minutes.

12. You're done - enjoy! Enjoy your kleftiko either eaten from the paper, or transferred onto a plate.

'The Life of Briam': **My Interpretations of Classic Greek Recipes.**

2. Gyros

The gyros is the King, the Daddy, *'o Pateras'* of Greek street food without a doubt and I would say that it is up there in the top three of the best street foods the world over. Yes, quite a claim but let me convince you …

Delicious, structured, spiced and really, really cheap - most gyros cost between €2 and €3.

One per person is fine, two even better. Have I managed three in a single sitting? Well of course!

Ingredients:

Chicken or Pork for the gyros meat (one large chicken breast or 350g pork)
Pitas/tortillas - 2 per person per serving
Red wine vinegar, lots of
Salt, lots of
Oregano, lots of
1 large tomato
1 medium red onion
A bowl of chips
Tzatziki (shop bought is fine, or make your own easily)
Paprika
Grease proof paper
Lots of napkins (optional, but strongly recommended)

Total Preparation Time: 15 minutes

Total Cooking Time: 15 minutes

Method:

1. Cut the meat into thin slices. Prepare a small flat tray by covering the base in salt and oregano. Then soak that in red wine vinegar -

don't hold back. Lay the slices of meat down and repeat with the salt, oregano and vinegar. Pile on layer after layer until you have no more meat.

2. To practical issues: for two people you don't actually need that much meat, maybe a large chicken breast or 350g of pork, but I always cook extra. Yes, the meat is key in this dish, but it is the overall interaction between a large number of ingredients, tastes and textures that really make these special.

It is possible that you can't get hold of the traditional round Greek pitas that are used. They sell them in stacks of 10-20 in the supermarkets here, but fairly good - and lighter - substitutes are the small Mexican flour tortillas for fajita/burritos/quesadillas etc that are readily available worldwide.

It is fine to leave that to marinade for an hour, but several hours or overnight is even better. There is no real need to turn the meat.

3. Once you are ready, discard the marinade and cook the meat how you like - on a BBQ or under a grill at 220 degrees for 8 minutes or so.

4. Prepare the accompaniments: slice the tomato and onion and prepare the chips.

5. To put your finished snack together, take a warm, round pita, onto which garlicy tzatziki is slathered. Then the meat piled on top. Then raw red onion, raw tomato and a small handful of piping hot chips. All that is needed to complete this work of art is a shake of paprika and then the gyros is twisted up in the greaseproof paper to hold it in place as you stuff it into your face at ever more crazy angles, usually making quite a mess in the process.

'The Life of Briam': **My Interpretations of Classic Greek Recipes.**

3. Pastitsio

The easiest way to describe Pastitsio is that it is a lighter, spiced version of Italian lasagne ... and I adore it. It comprises three layers, three parts, that if cooked properly will remain separate upon serving and for that you need three tricks of the trade, one for each layer.

A traditional Pastitsio has three layers:

A.   Bottom Layer: Pasta/spaghetti

B.   Middle layer: Lightly spiced meat

C.   Top layer: Rich béchamel

It would make sense for me to list all of the ingredients you need for each layer and then take each layer in turn, starting with the layers that take the longest to prepare

Ingredients For All Three Layers

A. Bottom Layer

Packet of pasta - I have seen just 'normal' spaghetti used, or penne, but really any tubular pasta, like macaroni, will do.
3 egg whites (save the yolks for later)
A good handful or two of Feta
Olive oil

B. Middle Layer

½ kg beef, ½ kg pork, both minced
2 red onions
1 large carrot
2 cloves garlic
Thyme
Oregano
Ground cinnamon

Ground cloves
1 glass red wine
2 beef stock cubes
500ml passata
Balsamic vinegar
A teaspoon sugar/honey
Worcestershire Sauce

C. Top Layer

100g Butter
110g Flour
Full fat milk
1 Onion, peeled, but not diced
Cloves
Bay Leaf
Handful of Cheddar cheese
Handful of grated parmesan
3 egg yolks (saved from earlier)
Ground nutmeg
Salt & Vinegar crisps

Total Preparation Time: 1 hour in total for all three stages

Total Cooking Time: 4 hours - 4 hours 30 minutes

Method:

The **Middle Layer** takes the longest - you can set this going and do everything else while it bubbles away.

1. Put the pork and beef mince together in a large saucepan and brown the meat. You should not need oil for this due to the fatty content of the meat.

2. Chop the onions, carrots and garlic and add to the pan. Add a really large shake of Worcester Sauce and the thyme and oregano.

3. Once the meat is browned add a glass of red wine and boil down. Then add the cinnamon and cloves.

4. A few minutes later, add the passata. Also add a spoonful of honey or of sugar as this takes away some of the sharpness of the passata.

5. Boil a kettle and dissolve the stock cubes in half a tea cup of boiling water, then add.

6. Season well.

You have now finished the hard work for the middle part. Bring to the boil then set on a low heat to bubble away, ideally for up to four hours, but if pushed, as long as the liquid has cooked down and the ragu is looking silky you can cut this down to 90 minutes/2 hrs.

Next in difficulty is the **Top Layer.**

1. Peel the onion and stick 10-15 cloves in it. Put it in a saucepan with the bay leaf and the full fat milk and bring to the boil. Once there, bring it down to a low head and just let all the flavours infuse into the milk.

2. Make a roux by melting the butter and adding the flour. Most traditional roux recipes have equal weights of flour and butter, but in this recipe because we want the overall béchamel to be quite sturdy we have chosen a heavier flour content.

3. Pour the infused milk into the roux using a ladle, one at a time, continually stirring with a whisk to avoid lumps. Add the cheese and the sauce should start to thicken up. Add more milk and, if needed, more cheese. You can never have too much cheese! Once done you should have enough béchamel to nicely cover the whole dish.

4. Season well.

5. One final touch is needed - add the three egg yolks that you separated earlier and stir. Then grate in some nutmeg.

Next, the **Bottom Layer**.

Once you have done this recipe before you can easily cut the cooking time down by doing both this layer and the Top Layer at the same time.

1. Boil the pasta in salted water for as long as the type of pasta you have chosen needs - this will be between 7-13 minutes.

2. Once done, drain the pasta and return it to its pan. Add a good glug of olive oil and a few handfuls of Feta. Stir.

3. Then add the 3 egg whites and stir. This, with the Feta, will help bind the pasta together.

It is now just a case of putting the layers together in a nice deep pan: pasta first, then ladle on the slow cooked ragu, then finally the béchamel sauce on top. I find it easiest done using a table spoon, working around the edges of the pan and then filling in the middle last.

This last part is optional and most certainly not authentic Greek in any way, but I like to add extra grated cheese on top of the béchamel and then crush up a whole bag of Salt & Vinegar crisps and use that for the final topping.

Cook at 180 degrees for approx. 45 minutes, making sure the top doesn't burn. I rarely see it served with anything else at all around here and that is because it needs nothing else. Just enjoy the majesty of the pastitsio itself!

'The Life of Briam': **My Interpretations of Classic Greek Recipes.**

4. Souvlaki

Smaller souvlakia are often served as street food in a similar way to gyros meat, in a 6 inch pitta with tzatziki, raw veg and maybe some chips.

While I love to order three or four of the small souvlakia in a taverna with some chips, there is also normally a larger souvlaki option on the menu, normally €8-€10, served with chips or salad.

I've had chicken, lamb, seafood and pork souvlaki and if I was forced at gunpoint to choose just one I would narrowly go for the pork.

The recipe needs souvlakia sticks - buy a huge bag from the supermarket, you will be amazed at how many things they are amazingly useful for - mostly in this house used for unblocking silicone sealant guns.

Ingredients

500g Pork (neck is most traditionally used here due to the fat content, but any pork will do).
One glass of white wine
Garlic
Olive oil
Seasoning
Lemon juice
Rosemary (chopped)
Thyme
Oregano
Greek yoghurt
Ziplock plastic freezer bag
2 large red onions
2 peppers
Souvlaki sticks

Total Preparation Time: 10 minutes

Total Cooking Time: 20 minutes

Method:

The freezer bag is the best thing here. It allows us to marinade everything equally without having to keep turning.

1. Chop the pork into rough one inch cubes and add to the ziplock bag.

2. Then add the thyme, oregano, chopped rosemary and garlic and season well.

3. Holding the bag upright, add 4-5 tablespoons of Greek yoghurt into the bag. This will help to tenderise the meat.

4. Add the lemon juice and the glass of white wine.

5. Stir well.

This is your souvlaki mix. Roll the bag to get rid of as much air as possible, seal it and place in a fridge for at least a few good hours, or overnight is even better. There is no need to turn the meat, just leave it be.

30 minutes before mealtime, start cutting out rough one inch shapes of red onion and pepper. You will end up with a load of offcuts, but I just save them for stir fries. These are your buffers to the meat.

Then on a souvlaki skewer add a piece of meat, then onion, then meat, then pepper and continue. Some people also use dry bread with the onion and pepper, as it soaks up a load of the juices and goes nice and toasty.

Squeeze out all the remaining marinade over the finished souvlakia prior to cooking - never waste taste!

These are best BBQ'd and enjoyed with a slice or two of lemon, but if you don't have a BBQ handy, then simply grill under a medium heat for 15 minutes, turning regularly. Wonderful stuff.

'The Life of Briam': **My Interpretations of Classic Greek Recipes.**

5. Kolokythokeftades (Fried Courgette Balls) with Lemon Dip

I have lost track of the number of people who have described favourite memories to me, of sitting by the sea in a simple taverna drinking barrelled, cheap white wine in the sun, with nothing more than a plate of these delicious morsels and a novel in front of them.

They are very simple to make, despite how long it might appear it takes to prepare. Around the Mani the most I have ever seen these served with is a slice of lemon, but I have worked out a simple lemon dip recipe. They are also absolutely gorgeous dipped in BBQ sauce, if that is not a crime around here.

Ingredients

2 courgettes
Red onion
Carrot
1 small potato
Handful of Feta
2 eggs
Handful of chopped fresh mint
4 tbsp of self-raising flour
Seasoning
Lemon juice and zest
Greek yoghurt
Olive oil for frying

Total Preparation Time: 45 minutes

Total Cooking Time: 5-10 minutes

Method:

1. Grate the courgettes, red onion, carrot and potato and put in a colander above a large pan.

2. Add salt to the grated vegetables and squeeze. The aim is to get all of the moisture out of the vegetable mix as possible and there will be quite a fair amount.

3. In a separate large bowl crumble the Feta, add the mint, self-raising flower, 2 eggs, season and stir.

4. After 20-30 minutes check on the grated veg and give them another squeeze.

5. Once you have got all the moisture you can get out of the grated vegetables, add them to the bowl with the feta and eggs etc. Stir. This is your mix.

To cook, just shallow fry the mixture in olive oil in the same way as you would for onion bhajis, so:

Put in a few inches of oil into a wok or a large bottomed pan and put on full heat. Use a small piece of potato to see if the oil is hot enough - if it floats you are in business.

Get a rounded off table spoon of the mixture and using a smaller spoon, carefully place it in the boiling oil. Rinse both spoons in water and repeat.

It depends on the size of wok or pan, but you shouldn't really have more than five keftades in there at any one time.

Each one will take 2--3 minutes to cook, then scoop out when ready and lay on kitchen towel to drain.

For the Dip:

Simply take the grated zest and juice of one large lemon and add to a small bowl of Greek yoghurt, with a pinch of salt and stir. Taste and add more lemon juice if needed.

Enjoy.

'The Life of Briam': **My Interpretations of Classic Greek Recipes.**

6. Spetsofai

Spetsofai is another homely classic, essentially sliced spicy mountain sausage (*'loukaniko'*) in a tomato sauce with peppers and onions. If you can't find authentic Greek loukanika do not worry, any spiced sausage will do fine as a substitute.

Serve with a load of crumbled Feta and a warm baguette for messy dipping.

Ingredients

3 Loukanika
500ml passata
1 large red onion
2 peppers, ideally different colours for presentation
Balsamic vinegar
Chili (chili peppers themselves, powder or bottled sauce)
1 clove garlic
Feta
Baguette (if required)
Seasoning

Total Preparation Time: 10 minutes

Total Cooking Time: 30 minutes

Method:

1. Grill the sausages for the required time and set aside.

2. While the sausages are cooking, slice the onion and the peppers into long, thin strips.

3. Fry the onion and peppers in a wok with a bit of garlic and as much chili as you like, the more the merrier in my view.

4. Slice the loukanika diagonally into thin strips of under 1cm in width and add to the wok.

5. After a few minutes, pour in the passata, add a good dash of balsamic vinegar, season and stir until bubbling.

Serve covered in crumbled Feta, ideally with a warm baguette to dip in the sauce.

'The Life of Briam': **My Interpretations of Classic Greek Recipes.**

7. Briam

This is often viewed as 'just' a side-dish, but I think that undersells the wonder of briam. Most traditionalists will argue that briam is just oven baked vegetables consisting of mainly potato and courgette, but it is far more than just a sum of its parts. As a dish it stands up well on its own and I like to take it several steps further by covering it in crumbled Feta and serving with bread to dip in the juices. It is also a great dish for vegetarians, just remember to swap out the chicken stock for veggie stock. I often make this when I have some vegetables that are looking a little tired, just to clear out the fridge.

It took a friend at a taverna to let me in on the two secret ingredients to this one. One of these is probably guessable, the other I would never have thought of.

Ingredients

3 large potatoes
3 red onions
3-4 courgettes
5 tomatoes
2 carrots
2 large peppers
2 cloves garlic
Olive oil
Seasoning
800ml chicken stock (2-3 stock cubes)
Handful of grated hard cheese (parmesan etc)
Handful of fresh mint
Feta and bread to serve

Total Preparation Time: 30 minutes

Total Cooking Time: two hours

Method:

1. Boil kettle and peel the potatoes, roughly chopping into 2cm cubes.

2. Boil the potatoes in salted water for 12 minutes and then put the kettle on again.

3. Heat oven to 180 degrees.

4. Slice up the other vegetables - onions, courgettes, tomatoes, carrots and peppers - and chop the mint, which is the real secret weapon in this dish.

5. Get an A4 sized deep tray and pour in a generous amount of olive oil and add all of the chopped vegetables, plus the potatoes, once ready and sieved.

6. Make the stock and add half to the tray, while scattering the chopped mint and grated hard cheese around the tray. These are the key ingredients.

7. Season.

8. Pop in the oven, centrally, and leave for one hour. Check after an hour, stirring and adding more stock if it is getting dry.

9. Put in oven for up to another hour, but check after 30 minutes to see if all of the vegetables are tender.

10. Serve with crumbled Feta and a baguette for dipping into the juices.

Printed in Great Britain
by Amazon

87329546R00194